WOMEN AT THE HAGUE

JANE ADDAMS

EMILY G. BALCH

ALICE HAMILTON

Women at The Hague

THE INTERNATIONAL CONGRESS

OF WOMEN AND ITS RESULTS

INTRODUCTION BY

HARRIET HYMAN ALONSO

University of Illinois Press

URBANA AND CHICAGO

Library of Congress Cataloging-in-Publication Data
Addams, Jane, 1860–1935.
Women at the Hague : the International Congress of
Women and its results / Jane Addams, Emily G. Balch,
and Alice Hamilton ; introduction by
Harriet Hyman Alonso.
p.   cm.
Includes bibliographical references (p.) and index.
ISBN 0-252-02888-0 (cloth : alk. paper)
ISBN 0-252-07156-5 (paper : alk. paper)
1. Women's International League for Peace and Freedom.
Congress (1st : 1915 : Hague, Netherlands) 2. World War,
1914–1918—Peace. 3. Women and peace—History—20th
century. 4. Women in politics—History—20th century.
I. Balch, Emily Greene, 1867–1961. II. Hamilton, Alice,
1869–1970. III. Title.
D613.A43   2003B
940.3'12'082—dc21   2003007102

Contents

Introduction to the Illinois Edition

HARRIET HYMAN ALONSO

✍ From April 28 to May 1, 1915, a historic meeting of women took place in The Hague in the Netherlands.[1] There, more than a thousand women from both warring and neutral nations of the World War I era came together to discuss their possible role in bringing about peace. By "peace" they meant not just an end to the particular conflict currently in progress but to all wars. The women who gathered were for the most part suffragists who met every other year through their organization, the International Woman Suffrage Alliance. Because of the war raging in Europe, however, the 1915 meeting could not be held in Berlin as planned. In its place, a group of women led chiefly by Aletta Jacobs, a Dutch physician and suffragist, organized the alternate International Congress of Women that resulted in the creation of the International Committee of Women for Permanent Peace. Jane Addams assumed the role of chair of the congress and president of the newly formed organization.

After the proceedings, two delegations were created to visit national leaders in an effort to promote mediation of the war. Jane Addams, Emily Greene Balch, and Alice Hamilton (functioning in an unofficial capacity) traveled throughout Europe as part of the delegations. When they returned to the United States, each wrote articles for various periodicals about their experiences. Those articles were then pulled together into the volume *Women at The Hague: The International Congress of Women and Its Results.*[2] To fully appreciate the book, it is helpful to have some background on the lives of the three women and the roles they assumed in the newly organized U.S. women's peace movement, which led to their presence at The Hague congress.

The Authors

In 1915 Jane Addams was already renowned for the establishment of Hull-House, the Chicago settlement that decided her reputation as one of the Progressive Era's most effective reformers and social thinkers. [3] Born on September 6, 1860, in Cedarville, Illinois, Addams was greatly influenced by her father, who stood out in the community as a great supporter of Abraham Lincoln and an opponent of slavery and was a God-fearing man who, his daughter claimed, favored Quakerism although regularly attending services in both Methodist and Presbyterian churches. Addams, therefore, was reared in a religious home that valued humanitarianism. As a girl, she expressed sympathy for former slaves and other impoverished people in the community. As many other children whose parents opposed slavery but supported the Civil War, Addams grew up aware of the dilemma between fighting a just war and maintaining moral witness against all violence. These values made her a perfect candidate for a lifetime of work around social justice issues. Her upbringing held her in good stead throughout her public school years, college-level education at the Rockford Female Seminary, and a period of searching for the kind of work she could do to serve both herself and humanity.

After visiting Toynbee Hall, a settlement house that had opened in London's East End in 1884, Jane Addams felt she had found her path. A year after the visit, in February 1889, she and her friend Ellen Gates Starr rented the semi-abandoned mansion of Charles J. Hull, once a country home but now situated in the slums of Chicago. There they created Hull-House as a settlement that would serve a predominantly immigrant community. Within four years of its inception the settlement boasted an array of clubs and functions as well as a day nursery, gymnasium, dispensary, playground, and cooperative boardinghouse known as the Jane Club. Lobbying and public campaigns launched by such Hull-House residents as Florence Kelley and Alice Hamilton resulted in an array of legislation, including passage of the first factory inspection act in Illinois in 1893, establishment of the state's first juvenile court in 1899, and investigations into city sanitary and health conditions.

While Hull-House made Addams a household name, it also resulted in her election in 1909 as the first woman president of the National Conference of Charities and Correction (later known as the National Conference of Social Work), her being the first woman to receive an honorary degree from Yale University (1910), and her being called upon to second Theodore Roosevelt's nomination to run for president in 1912 on the Progressive Party ticket. From 1911 through 1914 she also served as first vice president of the National American Woman Suffrage Association, and in 1913 she attended the convention of the International Woman Suffrage Alliance in Budapest, where she met many women she would see again at The Hague congress.

Three factors thus led to Addams's sensitivity to peace: first, youthful exposure to her father's ideals of social and racial justice and the fact that he passed along a humanitarian, strongly Christian identity; second, work with the poor and immigrant community at Hull-House, which taught her about commonalities among people and the importance of ethnicity to identity; and, third, work in the woman suffrage campaign, which awakened her to the specific injustices that women the world over experienced in personal, political, and economic arenas. Her ever-growing political clout and international reputation as an effective, respected organizer added to her attraction when other activist women were considering who should lead the new peace movement.

Addams's first foray into the world of peace was her membership in the Anti-Imperialist League, founded to protest the Spanish-American War of 1898 that resulted in an extended war in which the United States colonized the Philippines. She particularly deplored the racist and imperialistic language of the war, which referred to the "browning" of the U.S. population should numbers of Filipinos enter the country and by referring to "taming" and "civilizing" the Philippines, Puerto Rico, Guam, and Cuba (which became a protectorate of the United States) expressed U.S. ideals of white Christian superiority. By 1902 she began to formalize her ideas in print with *Democracy and Social Ethics*.[4] In this work, Addams made clear her belief that various ethnic groups could learn to live and work together and in the process develop a collective social morality that would eventually lead to cross-cultural understanding, tolerance, and the use of what now would be called conflict resolution or negotiation and mediation. As the democratic nature of living together became more embedded in local communities it would set the model for future national and international communities based on cooperation rather than conflict.

Five years later Addams wrote *Newer Ideals of Peace.*[5] Within that time it is evident that she had thought a great deal about the question of war and violence and begun her journey toward becoming a radical pacifist. As she noted in a "prefatory note," the chapters were based on studies in various aspects of city life (government, work, labor organizing, child labor, and women's roles) meant to show that there had been a "gradual development of the moral substitutes for war . . . in the industrial quarter . . . where the morality exhibits marked social and international aspects."[6] Addams's central idea in *Newer Ideals of Peace* was that working people, because they were in such close proximity to each other in factories and in their communities, had learned how to get along and depend on one another. Such intimacy broke down barriers of nationalism, language-isolation, religion, and cultural differences that were strong outside urban industrial areas. Once city-dwellers overcame hostility and shyness, they formed what amounted to a small, nationless state, almost a utopia of foreign relations. Doing so, Addams maintained, led to a natural abhorrence of war "because we shall find it as difficult to make war upon a nation at the other side of the globe as upon our next-door neighbor."[7]

That message, however similar to the one in *Democracy and Social Ethics,* was taken a step further in terms of peace. Addams pointed out that peace "advocates" had to make haste in moving toward following the example of those who lived in the industrial quarters and study and learn from them. Rather than trying to sympathize with people in poor and unjust situations, peace advocates and government leaders needed to look at the methods of communication that working people used and understand that people learned about "social justice, not only to avoid crushing the little folk about him, but in order to save himself from death by crushing."[8]

In other words, government leaders and peace activists should understand that there was much to gain by crossing class and ethnic lines and learning to negotiate the thin line that divides peace from violence. Indeed, Addams felt she received as much benefit from living and working at Hull-House as she benefited others. When leaders were educated in this "newer humanitarianism," nations would "as a natural process . . . reach the moment when virile good-will will be substituted for the spirit of warfare. . . . Owing to the modern conditions of intercourse, each nation will respond, not to an isolated impulse, but will be caught in the current of a world-wide process." The elimination of the warlike frame of mind, on which so much of U.S. society and the world functioned, could occur by ending militaristic culture in city governments, incorporating women who favored substituting "nuture for warfare" in decision making, and using more peaceful means of negotiating with labor.[9]

Naturally, Addams was distraught when war broke out in Europe in August 1914. In an effort to address the issue of U.S. neutrality, that September she and other Progressive Era social work reformers such as Lillian Wald and Paul U. Kellogg organized the American Union against Militarism (AUAM). The group's main concern was that war would harm its efforts to improve interethnic relations and result in fewer monetary donations. Addams supported the work of the AUAM throughout the war, but her personal commitment led her more to women's efforts, particularly because political work had recently introduced her to European suffragists who were among the earliest proponents of immediate negotiation among world leaders to end the conflict. Two Europeans, Emmeline Pethick-Lawrence of Great Britain and Rosika Schwimmer of Austria-Hungary, came individually to the United States to convince Addams, suffrage leader Carrie Chapman Catt, and other U.S. suffragists to approach President Woodrow Wilson about acting as mediator. In response, Addams and others called a meeting of representatives from prominent women's organizations. Held from January 9 to 11, 1915, in Washington, D.C., the conference resulted in the formation of the Woman's Peace Party, which in 1919 became the U.S. section of the Women's International League for Peace and Freedom (WILPF), an organization that is still extremely active.

The Woman's Peace Party was a uniquely feminist organization that sought to empower women. The preamble of its founding document proclaimed that women had "a peculiar moral passion of revolt against

both the cruelty and waste of war" and were weary of the "reckless destruction" caused by men in powerful positions. Women wanted "a
share in deciding between war and peace," and that share included
equality in all aspects of public and private life.[10] The preamble reflected Addams's deeply held faith in the power of true democracy and cooperation. Under her leadership, the number of Woman's Peace Party
charter members grew from eighty-five to 512 within a year. By February 1917 the organization's membership peaked at twenty-five thousand.

Among the women attracted to the work of the Woman's Peace
Party was Emily Greene Balch.[11] Balch's early years held much in common with Jane Addams's. She was born on January 8, 1867, in Jamaica
Plain, Massachusetts, and her father had a Union connection with the
Civil War, as did Addams's. As a result, racial justice was also a topic
for discussion in the environment in which she grew up. After attending private schools in Massachusetts, where she lived, Balch attended
college at Bryn Mawr, graduating in 1889 with a degree emphasizing
economics. She also studied political economy at the Sorbonne. The
results of her research were published in 1893 by the American Economic Association as *Public Assistance of the Poor in France.* Once at home,
Balch became entrenched in the work of Progressive reform, especially with women interested in working among the poor. In 1892, while
attending Felix Adler's Summer School of Applied Ethics, she became
friendly with Jane Addams and Vida Scudder. The latter, along with
Balch and others, the next year founded Denison House, a settlement
house in Boston.

Unlike Addams, however, settlement house work itself did not stim-
ulate Balch, whose primary interest was in the academic world. After
some soul-searching and further studies, in 1896 she accepted a position on the faculty of Wellesley College, where commitment to social
reform influenced her work and teaching on issues of the poor, immi-
grants, women, and racial minorities. In 1906 Balch openly declared
herself to be a socialist, a position that made her vulnerable to criticism by the college and local and national authorities. By 1910, however, with the publication of *Our Slavic Fellow Citizens,* a comprehensive
analysis of an immigrant community, Balch had established herself as
a sound scholar. She received a new five-year appointment as professor and chair of Wellesley's Department of Economics and Sociology.

After August 1914, Balch's and Addams's paths intertwined frequently. A pacifist since 1898, Balch, too, was deeply disturbed by the outbreak of war in Europe. As she recalled, "When the World War broke out in 1914, my reaction to it was largely a sense of tragic interruption of what seemed to me the real business of our times—the realization of a more satisfactory economic order. . . . Now all the world was at war, one hardly knew for what—for reasons of ambition, prestige, mutual fear, of frontiers and colonies. None of the war aims seemed very relevant to progress, in any important sense."[12] At first Balch took the same path as Jane Addams. She was active in founding the American Union against Militarism and establishing the Woman's Peace Party, especially the Boston and Wellesley branches. In the spring of 1915 she even took a leave of absence from Wellesley in order to attend the congress of women in The Hague. That event led to her full-time professional commitment to peace activism.

The third contributor to *Women at The Hague* was Alice Hamilton, daughter of a wealthy entrepreneurial businessman in Fort Wayne, Indiana, and reared in a traditional Presbyterian family that valued philanthropy and education.[13] Both her parents (particularly her mother) contributed great sums of money to community organizations, especially those addressing charity and the elimination of poverty. In addition, her mother was an early advocate of both temperance and woman suffrage, which introduced Hamilton to issues of concern to women. Her educational journey led her to an M.D. degree from the University of Michigan in 1893 and then to internships in women's and children's hospitals in Minneapolis and Boston. In 1897, after graduate work in bacteriology and pathology, she accepted a position as professor of pathology and director of the histological and pathological laboratories at the Woman's Medical School at Northwestern University. Hamilton found her life at Northwestern less than engaging. The Woman's Medical School was in decline, and she apparently had no colleagues whom she considered friends. Because she had been reared to value humanitarian efforts, Hamilton sought out Hull-House, where she became a resident and close friend of Addams. She lived there for many years and even after moving on returned often and for lengths of time until Addams's death.

Hamilton was most effective in putting her medical training and knowledge into practice at the settlement and became best known for her work in industrial medicine. Her pioneering investigations of lead poisoning in the modern factory system made her an expert in the field of industrial toxicology. The American Association for Labor Legislation sought Hamilton's advice in 1908 on how to achieve legislation concerning the issue of industrial diseases, and by 1915 she was an acknowledged expert on lead poisoning and other industrial diseases, an area in which she would work for reform. Her efforts made it possible for workers' lives to be improved by changes in work environments. More and more factory owners were compelled to install exhaust and sprinkler systems, provide medical examinations for employees, and adopt other measures to ensure worker health and safety. Hamilton also participated in work that once excluded women and even throughout her lifetime was open to only a few. She enjoyed breaking through these barriers yet also treasured life among the women at Hull-House, especially Jane Addams, Florence Kelley, and Julia Lathrop.

When Hamilton, "quite suddenly and I fear not on very noble grounds," as she put it, decided to accompany Addams and the peace delegation to The Hague in April 1915, she seemed to be outside her usual area of interest.[14] At the time, she had no expectation of spending more than three weeks away from home, one at the congress and another two visiting England with Jane Addams. She quickly, however, became engaged in the effort. On the trip to Europe, for example, she presented the U.S. delegation with a graphic lecture on the medical aspects of war. After attending other lectures, she read up on war in an effort to understand what caused nations to resort to it, something the other delegates did as well. She also became engrossed in political discussions on the ship and at the congress. Hamilton remained largely in the background compared to Addams and Balch. Her role in the postconference envoys was more as a personal companion for Addams than an official presence. She did, however, write an essay later included in *Women at The Hague.*

The Congress: April 28–May 1, 1915

The gathering of well over a thousand women (and a few men) in the great hall was an inspiring sight. Thirteen leaders, including Jane Addams, sat behind three long tables draped to appear as one.[15] Before them on the floor were eight vases of flowers, and large potted ferns dwarfed the women from behind. Addams sat center-stage, ready to act as a neutral and organized parliamentarian. Each woman represented a different nation. Each was intent on seeing that the International Congress of Women raised its voice "above the present hatred and bloodshed" and that however the women might differ "as to means" they declare themselves "united in the great ideals of civilization and progress."[16] Discussions were intense but businesslike. Although the chair allowed official translators time to help with English, German, and French, anxious participants and those who required translation into other languages created a constant din. Throughout the four days there were frequent outcries for silence, more volume from speakers (there were, of course, no microphones), and more time for translation. Yet in spite of the complaints the spirit of hope and camaraderie were great, and much was accomplished. Who were these women, and what inspired them to brave journeys through warring nations and cross dangerous seas to converge on The Hague during that contradictory week of dark war clouds and bright tulips?

Since 1906 the International Woman Suffrage Alliance (founded in 1904) had met in local groups and at international congresses to brainstorm and plot ways for women to gain the right to vote in their respective nations. Although the June 1915 meeting, scheduled to be held in Berlin, had to be cancelled, the suffrage network had such a powerful sense of connection that activists began to consider an alternate approach on how to use their caring relationships to address the current tragedy. The very personal violent and repressive effects of war combined with their experience as organizers to spur them to quick action. In this instance women who lived in the Netherlands, which was neutral, took the lead.

Aletta H. Jacobs, president of the Dutch Association for Woman Suffrage, and her Committee for International Affairs took the initiative and proposed a "business congress with no festivities."[17] Finding the initial response encouraging, Jacobs called a small preliminary gathering for February 12 and 13, 1915, in Amsterdam, where several Dutch women joined "four Belgian, five British, and four German women, so that one neutral country and both sides of the belligerents were represented."[18] The group planned the congress, decided on subject matter to be discussed, and appointed a subcommittee to frame resolutions.

Moreover, they stipulated that membership to the congress be open to women delegates from all-female or mixed-gender societies as well as to individual women. All participants were to adhere to two principles: "a. That international disputes should be settled by pacific means; [and] b. That the parliamentary franchise should be extended to women."[19] Furthermore, all in attendance were to agree that there be no discussion of national culpability for the ongoing war. All costs for the meeting were to be covered by the British, Dutch, and German women present, each of whom pledged to raise one-third of the necessary amount. Jane Addams's acceptance of the invitation to chair the proceedings boosted the planning committee's already high morale. Her name would signal seriousness and prestige to those who considered defying their governments' wishes and making the difficult journey— and for many the journey was indeed traumatic.

Addams, Balch, and Hamilton, for example, were expected to arrive four days before the meeting began, but they and more than forty other representatives from the United States were held up in Dover, England. Their ship, the *Noordam,* arrived just in time for the opening reception, but 180 British women were not as fortunate. Their government refused to issue travel permits for them until Home Secretary Reginald Mc-Kenna, under pressure, selected twenty-five of the group to travel. Only one of them, Kathleen Courtney, made it to The Hague. The other twenty-four were detained when all traffic between England and the Netherlands was stopped, allegedly for reasons caused by the war. Chrystal Macmillan, who had been in the Netherlands since early April, and Emmeline Pethick-Lawrence, who came in with the U.S. delegation, completed the three-woman team from Britain.

Closing the North Sea traffic prevented the lone French delegate (coming from England) from attending, and the German activist Frida Perlen was refused a permit to attend. Twelve nations, however, were represented: Austria (with six delegates), Belgium (five), Canada (two), Denmark (six), Germany (twenty-eight), Great Britain (three), Hungary (ten), Italy (one), the Netherlands (approximately a thousand), Norway (twelve), Sweden (sixteen), and the United States (forty-seven). In addition, 914 visitors' tickets were issued, and a number of day tickets as well. Expressions of solidarity arrived from women and organizations in Argentina, British India, Bulgaria, Finland, France, Portugal,

Rumania, Russia, Switzerland, and South Africa. Hosts of petitions came in from Italy, Norway, Sweden, and countless towns in the Netherlands. Together, the women in attendance created the International Committee of Women for Permanent Peace.

Missing, however, were many women from France, who explained their reasons for boycotting the affair in a "manifesto" from the National Council of French Women (Conseil national des femmes françaises) and the French Union for the Suffrage of Women (L'Union française pour le suffrage des femmes).[20] Primarily, they protested two "Conditions of Debate" that stated that "discussions on the relative national responsibility for or conduct of the present war" and "resolutions dealing with the rules under which war shall in future be carried on" were to be "outside the scope of the Congress."[21] Had they been consulted during the planning stages, they claimed, they might have been able to influence the group to eliminate these rules that so offended them. For years, they stated, they had collaborated with their international sisters on issues of concern for women, especially women's rights and the vote. But at present, they and neighboring Belgium were under invasion, and their most important concern was self-defense. Why, they asked, could the international congress of women not speak against the violence being perpetrated against them? If women's voices had been raised on their behalf, the voices were so feeble as to have gone unnoticed. The women in the two organizations behind the manifesto had no desire at present, they said, to support a unilateral pacifism they considered to be futile, even dangerous. Peace could not even be considered until at least the rudiments of international law had been reestablished. Although they praised the congress for its good intentions, they did not wish to break unity with their nation.

Although the manifesto was published in Dutch newspapers before the meeting, it did not reach Jane Addams until after the proceedings had concluded. As she noted to Mme. Pichon Landrey of the National Council of French Women, even had it arrived on time she would not have felt free to read it because it went against the stated rules.[22] Neither did she read a similar letter from the League of German Women's Associations (Bund Deutscher Frauenvereine) or those from individuals sympathetic to the French women's position. In her role as president and chair it was imperative that she not allow discussion of the war to take place. She wished, however, for the French women to know that those present had deep sympathy for them and greatly missed their collaboration. The manifesto, her letter, and those of a few French women appeared in the printed version of the congress's report.

The business of the conference took place over four days and began with an opening social reception on the evening of April 27. It ended at the close of the May 1 business meeting. During the day the women met to discuss the group's resolutions. In the evenings they attended such public sessions as "Women and War" and "Woman Suffrage and War." Business meetings were devoted to discussions on the various resolutions addressed here and in Appendix 3. In general, there was support for the resolutions. Much of the discussion concerned finer points of wording and grammar so the English, French, and German versions would all express the same sentiments. Without question, all agreed that women's voices needed to be heard and counted through the elective franchise.

Of greatest importance to all participants was that their protest "against the madness and the horror of war" reflect women's sensibilities (Appendix 3, resolution 1). Therefore, primary among their concerns were the "horrible violation of women which attends all war," the need for a permanent peace "based on principles of justice," and the unquestionable demand for political equality between men and women (resolutions 2 and 3). Two mechanisms could guarantee an equal voice: enfranchisement and representation in all governmental bodies worldwide. Although enfranchisement received its own resolution (number 9), it and governmental representation ran through the entire document.

A few debates, however, reflected the differences in women's antiwar positions. On the second day, for example, the women approached the topic of "Democratic Control of Foreign Policy." Alice Thacher Post of the United States suggested that besides asking that each nation make public all its existing treaties and conventions and that future ratification of such documents be in the hands of the legislative branch of every government, they should ask that "there shall be no war except one wished by the people of the world."[23] In other words, there should be no secrets between a government and a nation's population. Rosika Schwimmer of Hungary strongly objected and asked that the group be polled on who objected to the legitimacy of the concept of war and who did not. "Yesterday it seemed as if we would unanimously say: we don't want any kind of war, whether democratically approved or not," she proclaimed to great applause.[24]

Chrystal Macmillan of Great Britain proposed a compromise. Because all present seemed to agree that each nation should publish its existing treaties and conventions, the group could approve that. The issue of democratic control of foreign policy, however, should be held off, especially because not all governmental bodies were democratic. As a compromise the body elected to divide the issues. Resolution 14 stated that all secret treaties should be "void" and those in the future involve the legislature of each government. Resolution 3 stated that foreign policies should rest on "democratic resolve," but immediately following was a demand for women's political equality with men. Resolution 8 on "Democratic Control of Foreign Policy" laid out the idea that in order for a country to be truly democratic, women would have to have equal representation with men. In the same vein, resolution 3 also stated that "autonomy and a democratic government should not be refused to any people" and no territory should be transferred from one country to another without the people's consent. Only in this way would all people in a nation have a say in self-government. The result of the debate provides an example of the women's commitment to exactness and to ensuring that their final document truly represented the united voice of women. To that end, Jane Addams played the role of an impartial and organized chair.

A point of some debate concerned the proposed Resolution on Armaments, which expressed the concern that a strong profit motive on the part of arms manufacturers greatly hindered peace efforts. Emmeline Pethick-Lawrence protested the existence of what forty-five years later President Dwight D. Eisenhower would term the "military-industrial complex." Pethick-Lawrence claimed that "international agents" were employed by transnational arms corporations to "stir up troubles, to create rebellions, to manufacture panics, so that there may be a demand for weapons and munitions. . . by means of which they grow rich."[25] The proposed resolution urged that all nations agree to take over the production and sale of arms. The concern was to prevent mention of the role of neutral nations in the crisis. Elizabeth Glendower

Evans of the United States wished to have it stated that neutral nations should embargo arms sales. Addams, placed in what she considered to be the embarrassing position of having to "go against a criticism of her own country," suggested that the wording point to a future international agreement in which all nations (rather than individual nations) would control weapons trading.[26]

The women decided on two ways in which to achieve their dual goals of peace and equality. The first involved creating a "society of nations" that would include a permanent international court of justice. The organization would hold regular meetings "in which women should take part" to discuss and mediate disagreements among nations (resolution 11). One participant predicted that the court would become a place where issues that "threaten to disturb the peace of the world" would be placed before a judge who would exert appropriate pressure.[27] The group as a whole adjusted this to be a "permanent Council of Conciliation and Investigation," that is, a fact-finding body that would make recommendations for the settlement of conflicts. Until such an international body could be constructed, the women resolved to ask nations neutral in the current conflict "to take immediate steps to create a conference of neutral nations which shall without delay offer continuous mediation" (resolution 4). The idea had heartfelt support. As Rosika Schwimmer put it, "We must not forget, that we are not here only to speak, and only to make words, but that we want to lead to action."[28] Emmeline Pethick-Lawrence (from an "enemy" country to Schwimmer's Hungary) supported her colleague: "We can choose between different kinds of peace: a peace that is based on public justice, a peace that is based on democratic liberty, a peace that is constructive, a peace that is permanent, a peace that can be brought about through negotiation with all and by agreement with others. That is one peace, and the other peace is a peace formed upon exhaustion, on the battlefield of misery and despair, a peace that is founded on the victory of physical force."[29]

How to include "women's voices" in the peace settlement was a tricky issue, however. Resolution 18 stated that representatives "of the people," including women, should take part in the postwar peace settlement conference. In the meantime, however, how could the women try to ensure that would happen? Chrystal Macmillan moved that an "International Meeting of Women be held in the same place and at the same time" as the nations' peace settlement meeting.[30] When C. A. De Jong van Beek en Donk Kluyver of the Netherlands protested that the peace work should not exclude men, the phrase "representatives of the people" was added. Otherwise, the idea passed as resolution 19.

Rosika Schwimmer then proposed what became the most controversial of the resolutions: The congress should send "delegate envoys to carry the message expressed in the Congress Resolutions to the rulers of the belligerent and neutral nations of Europe and to the President of the United States" (resolution 20). As Elisabeth Bugge-Waern of Sweden remarked, "I am sure you will not receive any answer to the resolutions if you do not go and present them yourselves personally to the kings."[31] Representatives of all nations represented at the congress supported Schwimmer's resolution, certain that sending their message through the mail would only result in silence from world leaders. Kathleen Courtney of Great Britain, however, felt the idea would be impossible to carry out and that the women were allowing their hearts to dominate decisions they should make with their minds. To that Schwimmer shot back, "Brains—they say—have ruled the world till today. If brains have brought us to what we are in now, I think it is time to allow also our hearts to speak. When our sons are killed by millions, let us, mothers, only try to do good by going to kings and emperors, without any danger than a refusal." Her comments received a fervent "Hear, Hear, Hear!"[32] Resolution 20 reflected Schwimmer's idea. Envoys composed of women from both neutral and belligerent nations were to be appointed by the congress and report back so the women could plan further action.

The Language of Women at The Hague Congress

The women who attended the Hague congress were, in general, white middle- and upper-class individuals who had been active in the suffrage movement, women's club activities, labor or social reform organizing, and peace activism. Most were in their middle years, a number were single, and several (including those who were married) had chosen not to have children. As a group, however, they expressed themselves in the gendered language of women, laced with terms and images that separated them from the public posturing of male diplomats.

The 1915 *Report,* which records formally prepared statements, im-promptu comments, and letters, gives an idea of the common use of a women's language within the movement. The foreword by Emily Hob-house of England aptly sets the tone. "From the very moment of the declaration of War," she begins, "the hearts of women leapt to their sister women, and the germ of the idea . . . that the women of the world must come to that world's aid, was silently and spontaneously con-ceived and lay in embryo in the hearts of many."[33] The image of wom-en conceiving and incubating a life-affirming move to save the male world from self-destruction gave birth to the work of the congress. "In the quiet Dutch town [The Hague] amid the women of faith, Peace appeared again upon Earth and became a living force. Nurtured by womanly love and wisdom, she burst her swaddling bands, and with wide spread wings sweeping the world wrought as by miracle a subtle change in the universal attitude."[34]

The Hague congress's report is filled with images of women as vic-tims of war, protesting mothers of sons who were fighting the war, and logical, clear-headed voices that can bring the horror and bloodshed to an end would only men in power listen. In the "Address of Wel-come," Aletta Jacobs expressed the women's common grief for "the poor mothers bereft of their sons" and "the thousands of young wid-ows and fatherless children" left to fend for themselves.[35] The congress had been called because "the mother-heart of woman" had too long "suffered in silence."[36] Jacobs pointed out that men looked at war in terms of economics (especially in the profit that could be gained from commerce and industry) and the enhancement of power. Women, however, saw war as a loss of fathers, brothers, husbands, and sons. It was nothing but "pain and misery . . . not worth the bloodshed and tears." Women valued the sanctity of life far more than men did. It was part of the "virtue of our womanhood."[37] What women at The Hague congress could offer was a unique ability to remain calm when men could not and to "plan means and to produce conditions" to avoid future wars.[38] Of course, the vote was a mandatory piece of that for-mula. Because the male "half of humanity" had failed to come up with a way to settle international disputes it became "the sacred duty of every woman" to step up to the challenge.[39] Being able to vote and be a member of their governments would enable women to lead men to places they had as yet been unable to go.

In her presidential address at the congress's conclusion, Addams also drummed home the message that women were different from men because they were more rational and had a closer tie to the specialness of life. Addams expressed "sincere admiration," especially for representatives from the belligerent nations. They had ventured far from home during troubled times and yearned for peace when such expressions went against the policies of their governments and the wishes of many sister citizens. Addams referred to the "solidarity" of the women and their sense of internationalism.[40] "It is possible," she stressed, "that the appeals for the organization of the world upon peaceful lines have been made too exclusively to the man's reason." Now it was time to look to women whose "urgings to foster life and to protect the helpless" had prepared them for this important work.[41] Furthermore, if women did not step forward and act, those injured might accuse them of refusing "to assert clearly and courageously the sanctity of human life, the reality of the things of the spirit."[42]

The resolutions the group adopted also reflected the women's concern for other women as "victims" of war who suffer a "horrible violation" different from that of men's (resolution 2). Although the document did not explicitly spell out what "violence against women" meant, the *1915 Report* contains a poignant letter from the Abraham Lincoln Centre of Chicago's class in religion, submitted by four women (Martha C. Damier, Olive Cole Smitt, Cattie V. Whitcomb, and Ida S. Randael) and one man (Jenkin Lloyd Jones, the minister of the All Souls Church):

> That some action be taken to insure protection to women and girls from the horrible outrages from men of all nations in all countries, in time of war. The violation of women is, and always has been, one of the chief atrocities accompanying and following war, and men have not placed and will not place this outrage on a par with the desecration of personal property until women assembled in conclave as you are now, demand it. When humanity is served by the sacrifice of women's hearts or bodies, such sacrifice is gladly made. But in the wanton violation of women all humanity is out-

raged, ideals slowly built up through the ages are cast aside, and woman is simply regarded as the female of the species, as booty belonging to the victor.

In the name of home and childhood, of motherhood and human advancement, we demand that the violation of women be condemned as the most uncivilized relic of barbarous warfare and unworthy the soldier of any nation calling itself either civilized or Christian.

When the eyes of the civilized world are upon you and the ears of civilization are open to your utterances, we beg you to deplore and condemn the violation of women and to demand protection for our sisters of all races. We pray your conference to speak out, voicing the age-long horror and fear of women of America, Asia, Africa and Europe, in the hope that later, men gathered in official conference at the Hague may also condemn and take action to protect the mothers of men from outrage.[43]

Women at the congress referred to the "moral" pressure brought to bear on countries at war and indicated that women's voice in government would help define that pressure because women represented "one of the strongest forces for the prevention of war" (resolutions 2, 5, 7, 9, 15, 17, 18, and 19). Finally, resolution 16 stressed that children, those members of society most tied to women, needed to be educated and "directed towards the ideal of constructive peace."

Hundreds of letters arrived in The Hague in support of the congress. These, above all, reiterated the common bonds of sisterhood and motherhood. From Bulgaria came the message "amid the cruelty and the bloodshed, an image, bright and charming like an attractive muse, appears,—the image of mankind's mother. Amid the echo of the death-bearing weapons, amid the laments and moans of all humanity, a cry is torn out of the depths of women's heart, a cry against war." However, "This is the dawn of a new creative force, isolated till now, the dawn of woman's genius, the genius of love and mercy."[44] From the Swedish author Selma Lagerlöf came the opinion that "in future... women will recognize that their suffrage movement must also be a peace movement. As their social influence increases, so will their first duty be to protect the world from destruction."[45]

Carrie Chapman Catt, one of the best-known woman suffrage leaders in the world, echoed the sentiment that linked activism with motherhood: "O, my sisters, this, henceforth, is the especial task of the World's Mothers. . . . It is for us to foster Internationalism. . . . We must teach our sons and our neighbors sons that it is greater to live nobly for one's country than to die for it; that love must supplant hate and trust replace suspicion."[46] As the ultimate symbol of their role as mothers, Dutch women arranged for tulips to be sent to wounded soldiers in belligerent hospitals. Whereas distance prohibited flowers being sent to Austria-Hungary, Russia, and other nations further east and south, approximately two thousand boxes went to various hospitals in England and Germany and to interned wounded in the Netherlands.

The Text

The most noteworthy result of the congress was the selection of envoys who were to carry the women's message of peace and mediation to rulers of belligerent and neutral nations. Jane Addams, Emily Greene Balch, Aletta Jacobs, Chrystal Macmillan, Rosa Genoni, Rosika Schwimmer, and Cor Ramondt-Hirschmann composed the core group, which Ellen Palmstierna helped on a few occasions. In various formations they spent from May 7 through July 8 traveling through Europe. (The complete round of visits appears in the appendix to this introduction.) In tandem with the visits, local organizers of the International Committee of Women for Permanent Peace arranged for public meetings, study groups, and house-to-house visits to publicize the envoys' presence. Some of these travel experiences and perceptions became subject matter for *Women at The Hague,* which was written specifically for a general audience. The text was to describe the peace sentiment that existed among numbers of Europeans in spite of the war and counter negative publicity the congress had received. Although each woman wrote individual chapters, the book reads like a unified whole. Their voices are very much in harmony, and their ideas blend effortlessly.

Chapter 1, by Emily Greene Balch, presents her experiences onboard the *Noordam* in April 1915 and her days at the congress. Not wanting to pass up "even a shadow of a chance to serve the cause of peace," Balch took a voyage that may well have started her on the path to being a professional peace activist.[47] As she immediately points out, the congress represented the only successful effort on the part of international or-

ganizations to meet after war broke out. Other professional organizations, such as those of scientists, physicians, labor activists, and religious
leaders (in other words, men), were unable to gather their various members, who continued to divide along national lines. Although French
women had refused to come to The Hague, they still organized within
France for many resolutions worked out at the congress. Much of Balch's
first chapter describes the trials of her voyage from the United States to
Europe, the fear and frustration of being held "almost like prisoners of
war" onboard and "not allowed to land, not allowed to have any one
come aboard, and for all one day, Sunday, with no chance even to send
or receive messages."[48] Once released, the women hurried to the meeting, only to discover that others, primarily the 180 members of the English delegation, had not been allowed to leave their countries.

Balch emphasizes the woman-centered nature of the event, both in
the platform that called for women's voice in politics and in its possible effectiveness in exerting moral pressure on governments to negotiate a lasting peace. Although she points out her surprise at the negative publicity some of the press chose to give the congress, she believed
the meeting could provide a model for how people from various nations could civilly discuss differences as well as create ways to resolve
them. True patriotism and internationalism required bravery and clear
thinking. "What stands out most strongly among all my impressions
of those thrilling and strained days at The Hague is the sense of the
wonder of the beautiful spirit of the brave, self-controlled women who
dared ridicule and every sort of difficulty to express a passionate human sympathy, not inconsistent with patriotism, but transcending it,"
she stated.[49] Men, Balch believed, depended on the women to be successful in their efforts. Indeed, she claims (as did others) that soldiers
in hospitals frequently implored their nurses, "We don't know why we
are fighting. Can't you women help us? We can't do anything."[50] Wom-
en, the more moral, clear-thinking, and inventive members of society,
were the ones who could save men from destruction.

Alice Hamilton was not a formal member of either delegation, and
while others attended to the official business they were there to do she
took time to observe and speak to people in various cities along the way.
From her conversations she concluded that there was, in general, "no
such universal desire to fight on to the bitter end" as press reports had

insinuated. Moreover, because Europeans seemed unable to stop themselves from killing each other, the best path neutral countries could take was to try and help them out of the war.[51] Hamilton initially based her comments on conversations with various Germans in Berlin: a socialist who attacked the women for U.S. weapons sales to the Allies, pacifists who mourned the violent turn of events, and average people who believed that Germany was fighting in self-defense. Both in Berlin and Vienna, she juxtaposed the trials brought on by a shortage of food with the celebratory atmosphere of young men setting off for war. From Vienna the women traveled to Budapest, Berne, Milan, Rome, Paris, and London. Everywhere they went they heard a mixture of patriotic jingoistic expressions intermingled with a regret over war. Hamilton, however, had the impression that war fever was fueled more by U.S. travelers in Europe than by Europeans themselves. "There is something very distasteful in this," she stated.[52]

Jane Addams begins the most serious discussion of war in chapter 3, "The Revolt against War." There she describes the reactions of young men to the military. Although the women continuously heard that there was general consensus in each nation about their country fighting in self-defense, they came to realize that large numbers of soldiers and civilians had a strong desire for peace. Addams focuses on one group whose perceptions would later reverberate throughout U.S. press reports and cause disfavor among many who had previously adored her. After much observation, she relates that in each belligerent nation a group of young men existed who "did not want war" and blamed its existence on "older men" in high positions in the church and governments, who did not have to participate in the actual fighting themselves. Many of these younger men were soldiers "in the trenches convinced that war was not a legitimate method of settling international disputes."[53]

Although Addams acknowledges that many other men did not take this viewpoint, she felt it important to describe the generation and class gap. The younger men's perception, she believed, was caused by their world being a more international one than their fathers' and grandfathers' had been. They had met and studied or lived with people from many different nations and did not embrace the same sense of nationalism that older men did. The desire to avoid the violence of war was so great that there were men who would not shoot directly at enemy soldiers but would either aim away from them or shoot so as not to kill them. After speaking with nurses in hospitals, with wounded soldiers, and with mothers of men on furlough, Addams came away with the belief that there were "surprising numbers of young men who will not do any fatal shooting because they think that no one has the right to command them to take human life."[54]

Addams's most controversial comment, however, concerned the use of bayonets. One wounded soldier, she reports, claimed that bayonet charges were mad. "'Men must be brought to the point by stimulants and once the charge is begun they are like insane men,' he said." Addams then explains that women in several countries had been told that "stimulants" were issued to soldiers before a bayonet charge was ordered in order to enhance the sensation of revenge.[55] Addams's revelation, both in the book and in a public address at New York's Carnegie Hall given in July soon after she returned home, aroused the ire of the press and the public. She was accused of insulting the bravery of soldiers by claiming that they were cowardly unless given drugs. Although she tried to explain that she was reporting what she heard, many in the United States came to perceive her as a threat to patriotism.

In chapter 4, Addams singles out the press for a discussion of the dangers to free speech and the democratic process in nations where war is an everyday reality. Most important, the press in general, she maintains, tended to favor war and to incite what Addams termed "fanatical patriotism."[56] Peace sentiments or suggestions for terms of settlement were not reported in newspapers. Therefore, the general population knew only about the most sensationalistic aspects of the fighting or the ideas put forth by those government leaders most in favor of the war. Addams came away from Europe feeling that "the next revolution against tyranny would have to be a revolution against the unscrupulous power of the press."[57] Because people of the warring nations did not have access to various discussions on the war and its possible resolution, they believed that any nation asking for negotiations would be perceived as weak and therefore easily victimized by a stronger, more aggressive enemy. Addams's unfavorable analysis of the press may very well have fueled its sense of vengeance against her.

Emily Greene Balch (chapter 5) describes the envoys' visits to specific leaders and meetings with officers of such organizations as the

National Council of Peace, the League of Peace and Freedom, the Pacifist Philosophy of Life, and the Fellowship of Reconciliation, all in London, as well as discussions with other peace leaders. Local branches of the International Committee of Women for Permanent Peace were being organized in all the countries she visited, including France, Germany, Hungary, England, Scandinavia, and Russia. As the *1915 Report* indicates, the 180 English women who had been prohibited from attending the congress attended a local meeting where the congress resolutions were officially accepted. Three thousand Hungarian women became dues-paying members of that country's national branch. In Sweden, women's meetings were held on June 27 in 343 different locations.[58] Balch was heartened by the outpouring of efforts to encourage the European governmental leaders to talk to one another. Thinking about these leaders inspired her in chapter 6 to reflect on democracy and imperialism. As a socialist, an anti-imperialist, and a feminist, it is therefore interesting, and indicative of her time, that Balch, in summing up various effects of war (e.g., economic bankruptcy, labor unrest, and depletion of "racial stock"), adds, "The prestige of Europe, of the Christian Church, of the white race, is lowered inch by inch with the progress of the struggle which is continually closer to the *débâcle* of a civilization."[59] Yet this was the time to make peace, one based on democracy not imperialism and one that would grant people a say in the way they were to be governed. That was the civilized thing to do.

In resolutions listed in Appendix 3, the women protested "vehemently against the odious wrongs of which women are the victims in time of war, and especially against the horrible violation of women which attends all war."[60] The violations they inferred included rape, economic distress when breadwinners were killed, displacement from homes and jobs, the loss of children either as soldiers or from the collateral damage of war, psychological trauma, and physical harm. In "Women and Internationalism" (chapter 7), Addams discusses the growing movement of women from many countries and addresses issues concerning both women and men. Of the women who traveled through war-torn Europe in 1915, sometimes against the wishes of their nations and their families, Addams states that they "must have been impelled by some profound and spiritual forces. During a year when the spirit of internationalism had apparently broken down, they came together to declare the validity of the internationalism which surrounds and completes national life, even as national life itself surrounds and completes family life; to insist that internationalism does not conflict with patriotism on one side any more than family devotion conflicts with it upon the other."[61]

Addams partly framed her statement within the motherhood argument—women, who brought men into the world and nurtured them, experienced "a peculiar revulsion" when they saw them cut down in war.[62] In that way she could appeal to the broadest common denominator of women around the world. Addams, however, was not a biological determinist. As she made clear, "The belief that a woman is against war simply because she is a woman and not a man cannot of course be substantiated."[63] She recognized, however, that her greatest political tool for organizing large masses of women was to appeal for the well-being of their children.

Addams's final message was that the nations of Europe needed to start talking. If doing so necessitated outside help, then that help should be offered. In the end, if a settlement was reached that would make people feel that further wars would not occur, then perhaps they could accept the fact that thousands of soldiers had died to serve that end. (Of course, Addams could not know that the death toll would reach many millions before the war ended on November 11, 1918.) In addition, future democracy in the warring nations demanded the presence of women and workers as voters and within the government, especially as leaders. "Out of the present situation, which certainly 'presents the spectacle of the breakdown of the whole philosophy of nationalism, political, racial, and cultural,'" she concluded, "may conceivably issue a new birth of internationalism, founded not so much upon arbitration treaties, to be used in time of disturbance, as upon governmental devices designed to protect and enhance the fruitful processes of coöperation in the great experiment of living together in a world become conscious of itself."[64]

Appendix 5 of the volume is Julia Grace Wales's "International Plan for Continuous Mediation without Armistice."[65] Concise and to the point, the plan calls for an international panel of consultants to sit down and discuss possible alternative peace plans for as long as the war continued. The committee would consist of nongovernmental representatives who would have no ties to those in power and no authority to commit their governments to any plans discussed around the table. The plan has partly been adapted in the form of the nongovernmental organizations (NGOs) of the United Nations and in the work of citizen diplomats who form unofficial peace delegations to nations with which the United States or other countries are not speaking. Over the years, for example, WILPF and other organizations have sent delegations to Vietnam, Cuba, and the Middle East. Wales predicted that the long-term effects of the committee's work would be to end lengthy wars and open the "possibility of establishing upon a deposed militarism, the beginnings of World-Federation."[66] When the war concluded and the Versailles Treaty was signed, the women (at least initially) placed great faith in the fact that the document established the League of Nations and the World Court.

Peace Activities after the Congress

For Jane Addams and Emily Greene Balch, the Hague congress had a profound, life-altering effect. Both became entrenched in peace work for the rest of their lives. For Alice Hamilton, the congress meant embracing a pacifist outlook on life although professional work returned her to the world of health and science.

Soon after Jane Addams returned to the United States as first president of the International Committee of Women for Permanent Peace—of which the Woman's Peace Party was the U.S. Section—she spoke in Carnegie Hall and mentioned the use of stimulants before bayonet attacks. For years thereafter, and no matter how often Addams tried to explain that she had not accused soldiers of lacking courage but was reiterating what people had related to her, the episode was used to provide an example of the peace women's wrongheadedness. For weeks, Addams not only received scathing press notices but also numbers of abusive letters. Yet she was still admired as a social reformer. More important to Addams, her commitment to peace solidified during World War I. Her work with WILPF almost took precedence over her work at Hull-House, which was running along smoothly without her everyday attention. After she returned home, Addams paid six visits to Woodrow Wilson between July and December 1915. Her confidence in his possible role as mediator, however, dwindled as the president turned to a policy of military preparedness and then, in 1917, to war.

Throughout the war the U.S. Woman's Peace Party remained intact, although it cut back a great deal on activities and many branches lost members. The national office in Chicago remained open, but, Addams related, it was unpleasant to enter the place. "If a bit of mail protruded from the door it was frequently spat upon and although we rented our quarters in a first class office building on Michigan Boulevard facing the lake, the door was often befouled in hideous ways."[67] In order to find another way to continue her work, Addams volunteered to help Herbert Hoover's federal Department of Food Administration. She traveled to many states, urging women to conserve food and help increase food production. The work related closely to her belief in women's special responsibility to nurture the world and also to her conviction that peaceful communities would result if people worked collectively for the good of all. As she later put it, "I firmly believed that through an effort to feed people, a new and powerful force might be unloosed in the world and would in the future have to be reckoned with as a factor in international affairs."[68]

In May 1919, while world leaders were meeting in Versailles to write the treaty that officially ended World War I, many women who had met in The Hague in 1915 reconvened and formed the Women's International League for Peace and Freedom (WILPF). Their new constitution pledged the organization's support for "movements to further peace, internationalism, and the freedom of women."[69] Headquarters was established in Geneva, seat of the newly formed League of Nations. Jane Addams was elected president, and Emily Greene Balch was the first secretary-treasurer. Alice Hamilton, who attended the meeting as well, also accompanied Addams on a trip through war-torn France and Germany. When she returned to the United States she joined the faculty of Harvard University, the first woman to break through that male bastion of academia.

Emily Greene Balch continued her work with the Woman's Peace Party throughout World War I but was even more active in the work of mixed-gender radical pacifist groups situated in New York City. While on leave from Wellesley, she involved herself in three groups: the American Neutral Conference Committee (1915), the Emergency Peace Federation (1917), and the People's Council of America for Democracy and Terms of Peace (1917). Each group had evolved from the preceding one, and each reflected a stage of U.S. policies toward the war (i.e., neutrality, preparedness, and war). The three groups attracted an assortment of men and women—pacifists, socialists, feminists, and labor leaders. The People's Council, the only antiwar organization to be created after the United States entered the fighting, was particularly offensive to government leaders. They portrayed it as unpatriotic, even traitorous, because of its positions, which included support of the Russian revolution, an end to war, justice for conscientious objectors, and the end of poverty and labor exploitation.[70]

Because of her work with the People's Council, Balch was fired from the Wellesley College faculty. Thereafter, working for peace became her profession. Being secretary-treasurer of WILPF resulted in a move to Geneva, where she could work for peace, earn a living, and avoid much of the postwar Red Scare propaganda, some directed at her, Addams, and Hamilton. Addams avoided some of the persecution by making numerous travels on WILPF's behalf during the 1920s, hoping to inspire women to organize in Europe, Mexico, Hawaii, and several nations in Asia. Her inestimable reputation as a social reformer and peace leader made her welcome in many countries, while numbers of people at home gave her the cold shoulder.

As Addams grew older and her health fragile, she stressed peace as her work. In 1922 her book *Peace and Bread in Time of War* was published. In it, she again attempted to describe her work with the growing international women's peace movement, detailing her experiences at The Hague congress and during and after the war. Then, in 1930, she saw the publication of *The Second Twenty Years at Hull-House.* In that work she related her transformation into a global feminist pacifist. (Indeed, part of the subtitle of the book is "with a Record of a Growing World Consciousness.") Timely for even a modern reader was Addams's acknowledgment that she could not ignore the world's globalization, a phenomenon as exciting as it was challenging. "But whether we care for it or not," she wrote, "our own experiences are more and more influenced by the experiences of widely scattered people; the modern world is developing an almost mystic consciousness of the continuity and interdependence of mankind. There is a lively sense of the unexpected and yet inevitable action and reaction between ourselves and all the others who happen to be living upon the planet at the same moment."[71] That sense of interconnectedness had not been expressed until after Addams attended several congresses of WILPF and traveled the world on the organization's behalf. Until then, her global awareness had centered primarily on the United States and Europe.

After World War I Addams continued to maintain that society needed to take care of people's needs in order to achieve peace. Only the elimination of poverty, disease, hunger, and ignorance could provide an environment in which peace would survive and thrive. Women, predominantly, could foster that agenda. The League of Nations, the World Court, various citizens' organizations, and international agreements such as the Kellogg-Briand Pact of 1928 might all lead to the end of war. For several years, people who believed that Jane Addams was indeed a world peace leader nominated her for a Nobel Peace Prize. Finally, in December 1931, she was awarded the prize along with Nicholas Murray Butler. Her share of it, approximately $16,480, was donated to WILPF with the stipulation that the fund, should the group disband, would revert to the Foreign Service Committee of the Society of Friends.

Emily Greene Balch also continued to work for peace to the end of her life. From the end of World War I on, she devoted herself to WILPF and held important offices in the organization on both sides of the Atlantic. During the mid-1920s she traveled for the group to North Africa, the Middle East, and Central Europe. In 1925 she was part of a group of five women and one man that spent three weeks in Haiti as part of a WILPF task force examining the effects of U.S. military occupation, in effect since 1915, on living conditions of the native population. The result of the study, a book entitled *Occupied Haiti*, proposed the immediate removal of troops so Haitians could work for their own self-determination.[72] President Herbert Hoover's own later investigation reiterated the group's conclusions, and as a result troops were withdrawn in 1934. Balch was a constant author of WILPF position papers, whether on disarmament, the internationalization of aviation, the 1931 Japanese invasion of Manchuria, the need to reform the League of Nations, or a plea for mediation to end the civil war in Spain.

Once again, this time in 1946, the Nobel Peace Prize was awarded to a WILPF leader, who once again shared it with a man—this time with John Mott, leader of the Student Christian Movement and the YMCA.

Like Addams, Balch did not keep the proceeds from her prize. Of the approximately $17,000 she received, $10,000 went to WILPF; $5,000 was placed in a bank for a European colleague who had worked for WILPF; and the final $2,000 was used for the preparation and presentation of her Nobel lecture in Oslo in 1948, which she had been unable to give in 1946 because of an illness.

Emily Greene Balch lived to be ninety-four. At the time of her death she still hoped for the peace for which she had worked most of her life. One of the last entries in her journal reads, "I am bringing my days to a close in a world still hag-ridden by the thought of war, and it is not given to us in this new atomic world to know how things will turn out. But when I reflect on the enormous changes that I have seen myself and the amazing resiliency and resourcefulness of mankind, how can I fail to be of good courage?"[73] She died on January 9, 1961.

Alice Hamilton also lived a good, long life. Although not active in the peace movement, she continued to express her concerns whenever civil liberties were in danger, work for a healthy environment, and value aspects of peace and nonviolence. She died on September 22, 1970.

Jane Addams died on May 21, 1935, at the age of seventy-four. She had left instructions that her tombstone should read "Jane Addams of Hull-House and the Women's International League for Peace and Freedom." In *The Second Twenty Years at Hull-House,* she attempted to sum up her positive view of the efforts for world peace:

> In my long advocacy of peace I had consistently used one line of appeal; contending that peace is no longer an abstract dogma; that a dynamic peace is found in that new internationalism promoted by the men of all nations who are determined upon the abolition of degrading poverty, disease and ignorance, with their resulting inefficiency and tragedy. I believed that peace was not merely an absence of war, but the nurture of human life, and that in time this nurture would do away with war as a natural process.[74]

Attending the congress of women in The Hague in 1915 had led Addams and Balch to their work as peace leaders. As such, for them and for Hamilton, it led to new opportunities to help humankind. To read their thoughts on the conference and its resulting envoys is to gain more understanding of the development of these remarkable women.

Appendix: "Report of the Envoys to the Governments"
(Taken from *1915 Report,* 317–18)

The members of the different delegations appointed to present the resolutions of the Congress to the rulers of the belligerent and neutral nations of Europe and to the President of the United States of America
have been well received by representatives of the Governments in every
country visited. Although they cannot make any public statement of the
result of these interviews they are now, on the basis of the information
gained, taking further action.

The dates, the representatives of the governments and the names of
the envoys received are given below.

May 7th. The Hague. *Prime Minister Cort van der Linden:* Jane Addams. Dr.
Aletta Jacobs. Rosa Genoni. Chrystal Macmillan. Rosika Schwimmer.

May 13th. London. *Foreign Minister Sir Edward Grey:* Jane Addams. Dr.
Aletta Jacobs. Rosa Genoni.

May 14th. London. *Prime Minister Asquith:* Jane Addams.

May 21th. Berlin. *Foreign Minister von Jagow:* Jane Addams. Dr. Aletta Jacobs.

May 22th. Berlin. *Reichskanzler von Bethmann Hollweg:* Jane Addams.

May 26th. Vienna. *Prime Minister von Sturgkh:* Jane Addams. Dr. Aletta
Jacobs.

May 27th. Vienna. *Foreign Minister von Burlan:* Jane Addams. Dr. Aletta
Jacobs.

May 30th. Buda Pesth. *Prime Minister von Tisza:* Jane Addams.

June 2nd. Berne. *Foreign Minister Hoffmann:* Jane Addams. Dr. Aletta Jacobs.

June 2nd. Berne. *President Motta:* Jane Addams. Dr. Aletta Jacobs.

June 4th. Rome. *Foreign Minister Sonnino:* Jane Addams. Dr. Aletta Jacobs.

June 5th. Rome. *Prime Minister Salandra:* Jane Addams. Dr. Aletta Jacobs.
While in Rome Jane Addams and Dr. Aletta Jacobs also had a private
audience with the Pope on June 8th.

June 12th. Paris. *Foreign Minister Delcassé:* Jane Addams. Dr. Aletta Jacobs.

June 14th. Paris. *Prime Minister Viviani:* Jane Addams. Dr. Aletta Jacobs.

June 16th. Havre. *Foreign Minister of Belgium, M. d'Avignon:* Jane Addams.
Dr. Aletta Jacobs.

May 28th. Copenhagen. *Prime Minister Zahle: Foreign Minister Scavenius:*
Emily Balch. Chrystal Macmillan. Cor Ramondt-Hirschmann. Rosika
Schwimmer.

May 31th. Christiania. *King Haakon; Foreign Minister Ihlen:* Emily Balch. Chrystal Macmillan. Cor Ramondt-Hirschmann, Rosika Schwimmer.

June 1st. Christiania. *Prime Minister Knudsen:* Emily Balch. Chrystal Macmillan. Cor Ramondt-Hirschmann. Rosika Schwimmer.

June 1st. Christiania. *President of Storting Aarstad: Vice-President of Storting Lövland; President of Odelsting Castberg; President of Lagting Jahren:* Emily Balch. Chrystal Macmillan. Cor Ramondt-Hirschmann. Rosika Schwimmer.

June 2nd. Stockholm. *Foreign Minister Wallenberg:* Emily Balch. Chrystal Macmillan. Cor Ramondt-Hirschmann. Rosika Schwimmer.

June 16th. Petrograd. *Foreign Minister Sazonoff:* Emily Balch. Chrystal Macmillan. Baroness Ellen Palmstierna. Cor Ramondt-Hirschmann.

June 26th. Stockholm. *Foreign Minister Wallenberg:* Emily Balch. Chrystal Macmillan. Baroness Ellen Palmstierna. Cor Ramondt-Hirshmann.

June 30th. Christiania. *Foreign Minister Ihlen:* Chrystal Macmillan.

June 30th. The Hague. *Prime Minister Cort van der Linden:* Dr. Aletta Jacobs. Rosika Schwimmer.

July 7th. The Hague. *Prime Minister Cort van der Linden:* Dr. Aletta Jacobs. Emily Balch. Chrystal Macmillan. Cor Ramondt-Hirschmann. Rosika Schwimmer.

July 8th. The Hague. *Prime Minister Loudon:* Dr. Aletta Jacobs. Emily Balch. Chrystal Macmillan. Cor Ramondt-Hirschmann. Rosika Schwimmer.

The resolutions were also sent with a letter signed by the President Jane Addams to the Ministers of Foreign Affairs in the countries not visited namely: the Argentine Republic, Bolivia, Brazil, Bulgaria, Chili [*sic*], China, Colombia, Costa Rica, Cuba, Equador, Greece, Guatemala, Haiti, Honduras, Japan, Liberia, Montenegro, Nepal, Nicaragua, Panama, Paraguay, Persia, Peru, Portugal, Rumania, Salvador, Santo Domingo, Serbia, Spain, Turkey, Uraguay and Venezuela.

NOTES

1. Most of the background information for this introduction was derived from Harriet Hyman Alonso, "Nobel Peace Laureates, Jane Addams and Emily Greene Balch: Two Women of the Women's International League for Peace and Freedom," *Journal of Women's History* 7 (Summer 1995): 6–26, and Harriet Hyman Alonso, *Peace as a Women's Issue: A History of the U.S. Movement for World Peace and Women's Rights* (Syracuse: Syracuse University Press, 1993).

2. Jane Addams, Emily Greene Balch, and Alice Hamilton, *Women at The Hague:*

The International Congress of Women and Its Results (hereafter *WATH*) (New York: Macmillan, 1915). Addams and Balch each wrote three chapters, Hamilton, one.

3. Many volumes offer the basics about Jane Addams's life. I rely on the following for the backbone of my work: Anne Firor Scott, "Jane Addams," in *Notable American Women, 1607–1950: A Biographical Dictionary,* ed. Edward T. James, Janet Wilson James, and Paul S. Boyer (Cambridge: Harvard University Press, 1971), 1: 16–22; Allen F. Davis, *American Heroine: The Life and Legend of Jane Addams* (New York: Oxford University Press, 1973); and Jane Addams, *Twenty Years at Hull-House* (New York: Macmillan, 1910). I also employ the Jane Addams Papers in the Swarthmore College Peace Collection.

4. Jane Addams, *Democracy and Social Ethics,* introduction by Charlene Haddock Seigfried (1902, reprint, Urbana: University of Illinois Press, 2002).

5. Jane Addams, *Newer Ideals of Peace* (Chautauqua, N.Y.: Chautauqua Press, 1907).

6. Addams, *Newer Ideals of Peace,* vii.

7. Ibid., 19.

8. Ibid., 17–18.

9. Ibid., 26.

10. "Woman's Peace Party Preamble and Platform Adopted at Washington, January 10, 1915," Subject Files 463, Rosika Schwimmer/Lola Maverick Lloyd Collection, Rare Books and Manuscripts Division, The New York Public Library, Astor, Lenox and Tilden Foundations.

11. The skeleton of Emily Greene Balch's life is based on Barbara Miller Solomon, "Emily Greene Balch," in *Notable American Women: The Modern Period: A Biographical Dictionary,* ed. Barbara Sicherman and Carol Hurd Green (Cambridge: Harvard University Press, 1980), 41–45; Mercedes M. Randall, *Improper Bostonian: Emily Greene Balch, Nobel Peace Laureate, 1946* (New York: Twayne Publishers, 1964); and the Emily Greene Balch Papers: Swarthmore College Peace Collection, Scholarly Resources Microfilm Edition.

12. Emily Greene Balch, "Working for Peace," *Bryn Mawr Alumnae Bulletin* 13 (May 1933): 12, in Randall, *Improper Bostonian,* 135.

13. Biographical information on Alice Hamilton is based on Rebecca L. Sherrick, "Alice Hamilton," in *Handbook of American Women's History,* 2d ed., ed. Angela M. Howard and Frances M. Kavenik (Thousand Oaks: Sage Publications, 2000), 234; and Barbara Sicherman, *Alice Hamilton: A Life in Letters* (Cambridge: Harvard University Press, 1984).

14. Alice Hamilton to Agnes Hamilton, April 5, 1915, in Sicherman, *Alice Hamilton: A Life in Letters,* p. 184.

15. Thirteen women are in the platform photograph: Mme. Thoumaian of Armenia; Leopoldina Kulka of Austria; Laura Hughes of Canada; Rosika Schwimmer of Hungary; Dr. Anita Augsburg of Germany; Jane Addams of the United States (and president of the Congress); Eugénie Hamer of Belgium; Dr. Aletta H. Jacobs; Chrystal Macmillan of Great Britain; Rosa Genoni of Italy; Alla Kleman of Sweden; Thora Daugaard of Denmark; and Louise Keilhau of Norway. The photograph

faces page 2 of *Report of the International Congress of Women at The Hague, 28th April–May 1st, 1915* (Amsterdam: International Women's Committee for Permanent Peace, 1915) (hereafter *1915 Report*).

16. *1915 Report*, 35.

17. Ibid., xxxviii. A side trip to Haarlem to view the fields of tulips and hyacinths was offered on Saturday, after the business of the conference had ended.

18. Ibid., xxxix. The better-known of those attending were Anita Augsburg and Lida Gustava Heymann of Germany; Kathleen Courtney, Chrystal Macmillan, and Catherine Marshall of Great Britain; and Mia Boissevain, Aletta Jacobs, Rosa Manus, and M. van Wulfflen Palthe-Broese van Groenou of the Netherlands.

19. Ibid., 33.

20. Ibid., 313–14 (for the manifesto in French).

21. Ibid., 33–34.

22. Ibid., 314–15 (Jane Addams's letter in French).

23. Ibid., 96.

24. Ibid., 97.

25. Ibid., 121.

26. Ibid., 122–23.

27. Ibid., 89.

28. Ibid., 154.

29. Ibid., 156.

30. Ibid., 161.

31. Ibid., 171.

32. Ibid., 174.

33. Ibid., ix.

34. Ibid., xi.

35. Ibid., 5.

36. Ibid., 6.

37. Ibid., 6.

38. Ibid., 7.

39. Ibid., 8.

40. Ibid., 19.

41. Ibid., 21.

42. Ibid., 22.

43. Ibid., 304–5.

44. Ibid., 187.

45. Ibid., 222.

46. Ibid., 225.

47. *WATH*, 1.

48. Ibid., 5.

49. Ibid., 15.

50. Ibid., 21.

51. Ibid., 53.

52. Ibid., 49.

53. Ibid., 59.

54. Ibid., 70.

55. Ibid., 73.

56. Ibid., 87.

57. Ibid., 91.

58. *1915 Report*, 321–23.

59. *WATH*, 122.

60. Ibid., 150.

61. Ibid., 125–26.

62. Ibid., 128.

63. Ibid., 128.

64. Ibid., 141.

65. Ibid., 167–71.

66. Ibid., 169.

67. Jane Addams, *Peace and Bread in Time of War,* introduction by Katherine Joslin (1922, reprint, Urbana: University of Illinois Press, 2002), 73.

68. Jane Addams, *The Second Twenty Years at Hull-House, September 1909 to September 1929* (New York: Macmillan, 1930), 144.

69. "Report of the International Congress of Women, Zurich, May 12–17, 1919," in Marie Louise Degen, *The History of the Woman's Peace Party 1939,* reprint (New York: Garland Publishing, 1972), 232.

70. For more on the People's Council, see Harriet Hyman Alonso, "Gender and Peace Politics in the First World War United States: The People's Council of America" in *The International History Review* 19 (Feb. 1997): 83–102.

71. Addams, *Second Twenty Years at Hull-House,* 7.

72. Emily Greene Balch, *Occupied Haiti* (New York: Writers' Publishing, 1927).

73. Journal in Randall, *Improper Bostonian,* 443.

74. Addams, *Second Twenty Years at Hull-House,* 35.

Women at The Hague

Prefatory Note

The following pages give an account of the International Congress of Women, convened at The Hague in April, 1915, and of the journeys undertaken by two delegations from that Congress.

Much of the material has already appeared in *The Survey,* and is obviously journalistic in character. It may be of value, however, during these days of much war correspondence, as a report of European conditions from the point of view of that peace sentiment which survives in the midst of every war, but which is not easily uncovered.

If an apology were needed for putting such slight material into a book, it may be stated that the widespread interest in the separate articles seemed to justify presenting them in convenient form.

It is further hoped that this recital by three American women may correct the impression made upon the public by the contradictory accounts given through the press, and that the reader may become interested in the official report of the Congress.

1

Journey and Impressions
of the Congress

EMILY G. BALCH

𝕾 When[1] I sailed on the *Noordam* in April with the forty-two other American delegates to the International Congress of Women at The Hague, it looked doubtful to me, as it did to many others, how valuable the meeting could be made. I felt, however, that even a shadow of chance to serve the cause of peace could not to-day be refused.

Never have I been so thankful for any decision. As I look at it now, the undertaking repaid all that it cost us a hundredfold.

In this world upheaval the links that bind the peoples have been strained and snapped on every side. Of all the international gatherings that help to draw the nations together, since the fatal days of July, 1914, practically none have been convened. Science, medicine, reform, labor, religion—not one of these causes has been able as yet to gather its followers from across the dividing frontiers.

The women, fifteen hundred of them and more, have come together and for four days conferred, not on remote and abstract questions but on the vital subject of international relations. English and Scotch, German, Austrian, Hungarian, Italian, Polish, Belgian, Dutch, American, Danish, Norwegian, and Swedish all were represented. The French, alas, have not been able to be with us, but on the other hand the French women have been the earliest to actually form their national organization in support of the programme worked out at the Congress.

Our whole experience has been an interesting one. Sunny weather

1. A letter, with additions and changes, written from The Hague, May 5, 1915, to the students of Wellesley College; printed in *The Wellesley College News,* and in part in *Jus Suffragi,* London.

and a boat steadied by a heavy load of grain made it possible for the forty-two American delegates to the Hague Congress to meet and study and deliberate together during the voyage. The secretary of the Chicago Peace Society, who had come with us, gave a brief course of lectures on peace questions, and after these were over we set about the consideration of the preliminary programme submitted to us by the committee at The Hague who were arranging the Congress. Some days we met morning, afternoon, and evening and we added largely to the contents of the programme as sent to us. We recommended the so-called "Wisconsin Plan" for continuous mediation without armistice. This plan, as formulated by one of our delegates, Miss Wales, an instructor in the English department at the University of Wisconsin, had been officially endorsed by the Wisconsin Legislature and recommended by them to the consideration of the Congress of the United States. We had just succeeded in working out our proposals by the time we sighted land, and it was well we had done so, for, though we were on the *Noordam* for five days longer, we were hardly placid enough to work to advantage.

We were first stopped one evening under the menace of a little machine gun trained full upon us by a boat alongside while two German stowaways were taken off and searched and carried away. If the proceeding had been staged for dramatic purposes, it could not have been more effective. One prisoner, with a rope about him to prevent his escaping or falling overboard, shouted *Hoch der Kaiser, Deutschland über Alles* before he stepped upon the swaying ladder over the ship's side; both prisoners in the boat below us, with hands held up above their heads, were searched in front of that ever-pointing little cannon, then the sailors carried blankets and cups of hot coffee to them in the hold. All this, lighted by the ship's lanterns, was just below us as we hung over the ship's side. Every now and then out of the darkness a new vessel drew up to us. At one time five were alongside.

At last we were allowed to proceed, but not for long. Next morning not far from Dover we were stopped again and there we were held motionless for four mortal days, almost like prisoners of war. We chafed and fretted and telegraphed and brought to bear all the influence that we could command, but there we stuck, not allowed to land, not allowed to have any one come aboard, and for all one day, Sunday, with no chance even to send or receive messages. When telegrams were possible they were severely censored, and no indication of our whereabouts was allowed. "All in the Downs our fleet was moored," the old song says, and so it was and so was the *Noordam*. Around us were vessels not only of the English fleet, but of every sort, Norwegian, Greek, Spanish, and plain "United States," all with immense flags painted on their sides. Despatch boats, torpedo boats, and torpedo destroyers rushed past, sometimes five in a string; a silver-glistening dirigible, probably scouting for submarines, was visible all one lovely afternoon. Once we saw firing, probably the shooting of a stray mine. Inshore gleamed the white and green of the chalk cliffs, and a cosy old windmill twirled its leisurely arms.

It was pretty, it was interesting, but as the days slipped by and the date of the Congress drew near and people spoke of possible weeks of delay, it grew harder and harder to bear. At last, twenty minutes after getting a telegram from Ambassador Page saying that he could do nothing for us, we were released as mysteriously as we had been stopped, and by Tuesday afternoon were landing in Rotterdam. The first session of the Congress was scheduled for eight that evening at The Hague. We got through the formalities of passports and customs, took the train to the capital city, only half an hour away, were assigned to hotels by a friendly Dutch Committee of hospitality, washed and dined more or less, and were on the spot—in time, after all.

Not so the English delegation, 180 of them all told. The Governments had granted passports to only twenty and even of these not one could leave England, as all traffic, including mails, was stopped for the time being between England and Holland. Happily Mrs. Pethick-Lawrence had come over on the *Noordam* and Miss MacMillan and Miss Courtney had gone to The Hague earlier and the three did yeoman service throughout the Congress. From France no women could or would come, from Russia and Servia none, and from Japan quite naturally none. From the other great belligerent nations Germany sent a splendid group of twenty-eight women, among the most impressive of whom were Dr. Augspurg and Frl. Heymann. From Belgium five women came a day after the Congress had begun. They were given an ovation, and one of the German members of the presiding committee moved that they all be invited to seats on the platform, and this was done. Among the neutral nations the Dutch were naturally most largely represented; it is not quite easy to say how many of those who thronged the hall were members of the Congress and how many were visitors only, but apparently there were about 1100 voting. The next largest group were the Americans, about fifty in all, for some eight had gone earlier than the party on the *Noordam*. Norway, Sweden, and Denmark were all well represented with respectively twelve, sixteen, and six each.

The Congress was too large for any of the rooms at the Peace Palace or the famous Ridderzaal and met in a great hall at the Dierentuin. In general the mornings were given to business and the evenings to public addresses, while the afternoons were free for committee meetings and, to those not so occupied, for making friends and seeing sights. The most wonderful of these were the tulip fields near Haarlem, great stretches of solid color. There proved to be so much to do that in spite of making very good progress at each meeting two extra sessions, one Friday afternoon and one Saturday morning, were added.

The programme and rules of order agreed on from the first shut out all discussions of relative national responsibility for the present war or the conduct of it or of methods of conducting future wars. We met on the common ground beyond—the ground of preparation for permanent peace.

The two fundamental planks, adherence to which was a condition of membership, were: *(a)* That international disputes should be settled by pacific means; *(b)* that the Parliamentary franchise should be extended to women.

This meant a very substantial unity of opinion, which greatly facilitated the discussions, and I think that this is perhaps a sufficient justification of the policy which has been criticised in some quarters of making this Congress a suffrage as well as a peace meeting. Some of those present at the Congress, some of the Dutch ladies especially, and many of us Americans, also, felt that the suffrage element was overstressed; but, after all, it was the question of peace that, out and out, dominated the discussions and focussed our purpose and interest. Yet I hear that many Dutch ladies went opposed to suffrage and came away convinced that if women are to do anything effective for peace they must have a voice in public questions.

A series of brilliant evening meetings were held during the Congress, at which the chair was taken respectively by Dr. Aletta Jacobs, of Holland, Dr. Anita Augspurg, of Germany, and Miss Chrystal MacMillan, of England.

On the first evening, Dr. Aletta Jacobs, the President of the Dutch Executive Committee, in welcoming the members of the Congress, expressed her appreciation of the courage shown by those women who had braved all the dangers, risks, and difficulties of travelling in war time from one country to another.

"With mourning hearts we stand united here," she said. "We grieve for many brave young men who have lost their lives on the battlefield before attaining their full manhood; we mourn with the poor mothers bereft of their sons; with the thousands of young widows and fatherless children, and we feel that we can no longer endure in this twentieth century of civilization that governments should tolerate brute force as the only solution of international disputes."

Dr. Jacobs proceeded to explain why the Congress had been called in the midst of the war instead of postponing it until the days of peace, and indicated how many more difficulties such an international gathering would present if it had to include representatives of both victorious and conquered nations.

"Although our efforts may not shorten the present war," she exclaimed, "there is no doubt that this pacific assemblage of so many nations will have its moral effect upon the belligerent countries. . . . Those of us who have convened this Congress, however, have never called it a PEACE CONGRESS, but an International Congress of Women assembled to protest against war, and to suggest steps which may lead to warfare becoming an impossibility."

The meeting was further addressed by Miss Lindhagen, a town councillor of Stockholm, Sweden, Mrs. Pethick-Lawrence of Great Britain, and others.

At the public meeting of the second evening of the Congress, there was not a vacant seat in the large hall. The meeting was addressed by Miss Holbrook, of Chicago, on the resolution which was passed at the preceding meeting as to the education of children; by Mrs. De jong Van Beek en Donk of The Hague, who showed herself master of the subject, on Arbitration and Conciliation; and by Mme. Rosika Schwimmer, who gave one of her most stirring addresses.

On the third evening the meeting was addressed by Miss Thora Daugaard of Denmark, Miss Kathleen Courtney of England, Miss Leonora O'Reilly of the Women's Trades Union League of the United States, by the President of the Congress, and others, including Frau

Lecher of Austria, who made one of the most touching speeches of the Congress. She had been in the very midst of the miseries of war for months in her own country, working in the hospitals, where she had seen the most intense suffering borne without complaint; but what was the use of healing wounds if they were to be torn open again?

At each of the evening meetings greetings were read from individuals and organizations, in many countries, including Bulgaria, Iceland, Portugal, Poland, Turkey, and from such women as Olive Schreiner, Ellen Key, and Mrs. Chapman Catt. More than three hundred such formal greetings were received, of which only a small portion could be read. About thirty protests were also received.

One of the most warmly debated questions was on Madame Schwimmer's proposal, which was finally accepted, to send delegates to the different capitals, both belligerent and neutral, to carry to them the resolutions voted by the Congress.

The programme that has been worked out is, I feel, a very able document; certain good authorities think that, profiting as it did by many preceding studies and congresses, it is the best peace platform that has yet been drawn up.[2] It would make an admirable basis for a brief study by an individual, or a club, or a little group of friends, of the problem of peace in the constructive sense. For what we are working for is not what our English friends call "damp angel Peace," not stagnation, nor quietism, not a weak giving way to pressure, but a world in which national activities reënforce instead of neutralizing one another.

A very curious thing has been the attitude of the majority of the press representatives who were present. Most of them apparently had been sent to get an amusing story of an international peace gathering of women—"base and silly" enough to try to meet in war time—breaking up in quarrel. Day by day they went away with faces long with disappointment. "Nothing doing to-day, but something worth while may happen to-morrow." In England the Congress was reported to be managed in the interest of Germany; in Germany the delegates were threatened with social boycott for attending a pro-British meeting; and in many countries the meetings were reported to have been either prac-

2. The official report of the International Congress of Women at The Hague, or copies of the resolutions, may be obtained from the Women's Peace Party of America, at 116 So. Michigan Ave., Chicago.

tically unattended or to have closed in a row. Nothing could be further from the truth than all these stories. The largest hall in The Hague was needed for the meetings, over two thousand often being present; and, difficult as it is to conduct business with so mixed and differing a constituency, with different languages, different rules of parliamentary procedure, and divergent views, Miss Addams and the other officials carried on orderly and effective sessions, marked by the most active will for unity that I have ever felt in an assemblage.

What stands out most strongly among all my impressions of those thrilling and strained days at The Hague is the sense of the wonder of the beautiful spirit of the brave, self-controlled women who dared ridicule and every sort of difficulty to express a passionate human sympathy, not inconsistent with patriotism, but transcending it.

The sessions were heavily fraught with emotion, it could not be otherwise, but the emotion found little expression in words. When it did, it was on a high and noble plane. There was something profoundly stirring and inexpressibly inspiriting in the attitude of these women, many of them so deeply stricken, so closely bound to the cause of their country as they understand it, yet so full of faith in the will for good of their technical enemies and so united in their common purpose to find the principles in which permanent relations of international friendship and coöperation can ultimately be established.

There was not one clash or even danger of a clash over national differences; on every hand was the same moving consciousness of the development of a new spirit which is growing in the midst of the war as the roots of the wheat grow under the drifts and tempests of winter.

Because there were no clashes along national lines, it must not be thought, however, that the Congress was stagnantly placid. People cared too much for the subject under debate for that to be possible. There were most vigorous differences of opinion over details, and some energetic misunderstandings, for which the necessity of translating each speech into two other languages supplied many openings, besides the difficulties arising from different parliamentary usages. One's every faculty was on the stretch hour after hour, and we wondered afterwards why we felt so exhausted.

I have spoken of the impression made on me by the friendliness of the women from the warring countries. Perhaps the next most powerful impressions were, first, the closer sense of the tragic horror of the war, of which some of the women bore the imprint in their very faces, not to speak of what they said; and, secondly, of the fear of the men and women of the neutral countries, lest they, too, be dragged into the pit where the other nations are struggling. The women who have the vote (that is, the Norwegian and Danish, for the Finnish women could not get to The Hague) showed an additional timidity—the timidity of those who are in a critical and delicate situation, and who, being themselves jointly responsible, have to take every step with the greatest discreetness.

Since the close of the Congress some of those of us who have been chosen to go as delegates to various Governments have called on some of the foreign ministers at The Hague as a preliminary step and some very illuminating things have been said to us. One of the ministers said the most important thing that we could do was to help to educate children away from militarism. Another deprecated all agitation of the subject of peace, as it weakens the energy for war in case war comes.

It has been a surprise to me to find how much this very innocent gathering has been regarded. I imagined that it might very likely simply be ignored. On the contrary, it gives considerable exercise to the minds of various belligerent Governments, and the great news agencies have found it worth while to invent all sorts of false reports about it, as I have said. Futile as talk seems, the way it is dreaded shows that it does have its effect. Ideas seem so unreal, so powerless, before the vast physical force of the military masses to-day; it is easy to forget that it is only ideas that created that force and that keep it in action. Let war once be disbelieved in, and that force melts into nothing.

Certainly the Congress has made its contribution to the beginning of a piece of long, serious, enthusiastic work which is to be done in every country and all the time; the work of "changing the mind of Europe," as Professor Schevill says, of creating and making general the state of mind which does not desire to profit at the expense of other peoples, which desires to decide difficulties by reason and not by force, and which replaces national and social prejudices by mutual goodwill and understanding. This attitude will express itself in opposition to armaments (by sea or land) and in a patient readiness to wait for the righting of wrongs by agreement.

In the distress of mind that the war breeds in every thinking and feeling person, there is a poignant relief in finding a channel through which to work for peace. The rehabilitating the wounded that they may rise and go to the front again, all that coöperates with the mutual destruction of war, absorbs energy and expresses sympathy, but it is not the work that many of us long to find a way to do. In writing and making available our forces,—our pennies, our time, our reading hours, our intelligences, our sympathies—we can coöperate toward peace, longing for which, as Lowell said,

> "our spirits wilt
> Like shipwrecked men's on rafts for water."

It is important to have a great reservoir of spiritual and intellectual energy, to have ramifications in every village and club and church, so that when the word goes out, "This is to be, done now," we can all line up behind our leaders and act in unison in all the countries of the war-racked world. Study clubs and peace forums and subscriptions and keeping oneself informed are humdrum matters, yet they too are hitched to a star, the star of hope in human destiny beyond the war clouds.

The Hague is such a preëminently civilized city—so tidy, so clean, so safe, so pleasant, so pretty. Man has done such wonders in subduing nature, in creating a world in the image of his own desires, a background for happy human living; and in every city in Europe essentially the same conditions exist for people substantially the same. In reality Europe is already, in normal times, one single society. Yet perfectly artificial national boundaries are made to signify collective greeds and hatreds, and only a few miles off the fields are permanently ruined, and the countryside is poisoned with corpses, and all the decent thrifty little homes are smashed to dust, and the irreplaceable beauties of the cities are destroyed, and living, thinking men are deliberately killing one another. The soldiers in the hospitals say to their nurses: "We don't know why we are fighting. Can't you women help us? We can't do anything." That is the very question we are trying to answer.

2

At the War Capitals

ALICE HAMILTON

☙ The delegations to the war capitals consisted of the president and vice-president of the Congress, Miss Addams of Chicago and Dr. Jacobs of Amsterdam. Frau Wollften Palthe of The Hague and myself, who accompanied them, were not official members of the delegation and usually took no part in the formal interviews with ministers of foreign affairs or chancellors; so that my account of our wanderings must be confined to the unofficial parts, to the people we met informally and the impressions we gained as we passed through the countries and stopped in the capitals and saw the life there.

There were absolutely no hardships encountered anywhere, not even real discomforts. Inconveniences there were in the shape of tiresome waiting in consular offices for passports,—a formality which had to be repeated between each two countries; but aside from that, travel was easy and comfortable. The first Government visited by the delegation was the Dutch, since the Congress was held at The Hague, and after that came Great Britain, where the delegation saw the minister of foreign affairs and other officials. During that week I was in Belgium, so that the experiences in London given later in this chapter were crowded into the week we spent there while waiting for our return steamer to America.

The beginning of our joint pilgrimage was on May 19, when with the two Dutch women we left Amsterdam for the day's journey to Berlin. Germany looked far more natural than we had been led to expect; indeed, the only unusual feature to my eyes was the absence of young and middle-aged men in the fields, where the work was being carried on almost entirely by women, children, and old men.

We reached Berlin at night and the next morning as we drank our coffee a card was brought up of a prominent Socialist, a member of the Reichstag and an authority on city planning, who visited this country some two years ago and spoke in many of our large cities. We went down to meet him, but seeing no one in the room except a few officers, thought there was some mistake; when, to our surprise, a tall, blond soldier came up and saluted and we recognized that this was he. We had never supposed that he would actually be in the army, though we knew that he was one of the military Socialists,—indeed, one of those selected by the Kaiser to go on a mission to Italy and try to persuade the Italian Socialists that Italy should remain loyal to the Triple Alliance.

We talked together and he told us of Italy's probable entrance into the war, insisting that it would be a matter of no military importance, but an act of unforgivable treachery. He had been up all the night before at the foreign office and his eyes had that dull hunted look that goes with sleeplessness and intense emotion. He was the first one to attack us on the subject of America's sale of munitions of war to the allies, an attack to which we became wearily accustomed before we left Germany and Austria. He was just back from nine days at the front and claimed that every shell which had fallen in that part of the line while he was there was an American shell. Nevertheless, he was most friendly and readily promised to do what he could to secure an interview for the delegation with the foreign office.

After he left, I went out on a few errands and got my first impression of Berlin. The city, of course, was in perfect order, yet the war met me on all sides. The walls were placarded and the windows full of appeals for money for all sorts of objects; for blinded soldiers, for the relief of the widows of the heroes of a certain battle, for a woman's fund to be made up of pennies and presented to the Kaiser, and—much the most terrible of all—long lists of the latest casualties. But there were no wounded soldiers to be seen and no evidence of poverty and suffering, the relief work is apparently well done. Later on, when we were taken around by one of the leading philanthropists of Berlin we saw how work has been provided for those who need it, for the women especially. I had a curious sensation on that expedition of having seen and heard it all before; and then I remembered that just a little while ago in Brussels I had seen gentle Belgian ladies organizing work for the Belgian poor in exactly the same way as these gentle German ladies were doing it for the German poor. Both in Paris and in London it was the same.

We had been told before we went to Germany that the people were absolutely united in a determination to fight until Germany was victorious, that there were not a dozen men the length and breadth of the land who were even thinking, much less talking, of peace.

Of course, such unanimity is inconceivable in a nation of sixty-five million thinking people, and it was easy enough for us to convince ourselves that it did not exist. From the first we met men and women who were pacifists. The one who stands out most prominently in my mind is the clergyman, who has gathered around him a group of people free from bitterness and from ultra-patriotism, fair-minded, and deeply sorrowful over the war. Many of them belong also to a group that calls itself *Der Bund Neues Vaterland,* which stands for very much the same things as the Union of Democratic Control in England,—that is, for a peace without injustice or humiliating terms to any people, no matter who is victor.

Of course we also met people who held the point of view which we in America have been led to think universal in Germany. The *Lusitania* was still in everyone's mind and the first note from America had just been received. I talked to many people who accepted the sinking of the vessel without questioning. She was carrying ammunition, she was armed, the passengers had been warned and had no more reason to complain than if they had deliberately entered a city that was being besieged. For instance at a tea one afternoon a lady of much sweetness and intelligence described how her three little girls had each adopted a convalescent soldier, and how they saved their pennies to buy tobacco for their protégés and gave them one of their three daily slices of bread. Then the lady continued in exactly the same tone: "And the day the news came of the sinking of the *Lusitania* we all took a holiday. There were no lessons, and we sent for our soldiers, and all went off for a picnic in the country." These people were absolutely sure that Germany was fighting in self-defence, and toward the invasion of Belgium most of them held the belief that it had been a military necessity, but that there must be no permanent occupation. No one believed in the tales of atrocities. "If you knew our good German soldiers, you would see how impossible all that is."

As for our selling munitions of war to the allies, the resentment it arouses is almost incredible. Many of them seem to suppose that all the ammunition used by the allies comes from America. The American wife of a German nobleman told us that a widowed friend had come to see her with a bit of shell which some soldier had sent her from the front, saying it was the shell that had killed her husband. And the woman had shown her the ghastly thing, and said, "Look at it and tell me if it is an American shell."

We stood up stoutly for our country, arguing that it was Germany which had prevented both Hague Congresses from pronouncing against this very practice, that Germany had herself invariably taken every opportunity to sell munitions to warring countries, that for us to change international law and custom in the middle of the present war in favor of Germany and to the detriment of the allies would be an unneutral act, but it was mostly useless. I think we convinced, perhaps, two or three men. Most of them did not even listen to our explanation.

There was no difficulty in securing an interview for the delegation with the minister of foreign affairs. During the interview with the chancellor I waited in a spacious room in the chancellery on the Wilhelm Strasse, looking out on a great shady garden right in the heart of Berlin. From there we went to pay some calls on men who we thought might throw some light on the question of the possibility of neutral nations acting as negotiators between the warring countries. It was very easy to secure the introductions we wanted, partly through German friends and partly through some American newspaper men.

We called first on a learned professor who did not seem to me either wise or just, and his idea of the sort of intervention which would be of value in this crisis was so utterly un-American that we thought it hardly worth listening to. Briefly, he advised that President Wilson should use threats to the two chief belligerents and thus bring them to terms. "Let him," he said, "tell England that he will place an embargo on munitions of war, unless she will accept reasonable terms for ending the war, and let him tell Germany that this embargo will be lifted unless Germany does the same."

Miss Addams told him that such a move would be impossible, even if it were of any value: that for the President to use threats would be to lose his moral force, and that he would not have the country behind him, But the professor waved aside as absurd both these objections. "Moral influence is nothing," he said. "What is needed is armed mediation. Your President has the right under your constitution to do this; he need not consult the country."

He went on to say much that he had already said in print; that Germany desires no new territory in Europe, but what she requires is colonies, and that he would be in favor of her evacuating Belgium on condition of her being given concessions in the Belgian Congo. He was one of the Germans who could see no argument in defence of our sale of munitions and who considered the sinking of the *Lusitania* absolutely justified. As we rose to go he said suddenly, "We learned yesterday, my wife and I, of the fourteenth of our near relatives who have died in this war." He sighed heavily—"There are others of course who are wounded and ill."

We found the most famous journalist of Germany very interesting. He is a little man with a big head, almost all of it forehead and hair, his eyes tired and burnt-out and his general aspect full of weary depression. People had warned us against him, calling him a fire-eater, one of the men who had done most to encourage the war. To us he seemed quite the contrary; he seemed to regard it as a terrible tragedy. He was very fair to our country, saying that Germany had no right to criticise our sale of ammunition to the allies. He said he had always told the Germans that since they had a great advantage in their enormous factories at Essen, England naturally must strive to offset it by an equal advantage, and this she had in her navy, which enabled her to buy the supplies she could not manufacture. He said it was poor sportsmanship for Germany to protest. As for help from the neutral nations in this crisis, he seemed to think it the only hope, and yet not an immediate hope.

The most moving and impressive interviews I recall in Germany were first one with a young German soldier full of a sick horror of war, the other with a former Government official in Berlin, whom we went to see just after our conversation with the journalist. This man had known and loved England and he had believed that the two countries had come to understand each other much better during the last few years and that he had helped to bring this about. Then came those terrible days in July and he had struggled against the men who were making the war, but he had gone down to defeat seeing all he had worked for vanish in a week when his beloved country determined on a course which to him could seem only a hideous blunder. He was so wretched that as he talked to us he would every now and then drop his head in his hands and fall into silence, then suddenly look up and say: "You know I am no longer in the Government, I am discredited, suspected, an outcast," or, "They may say what they will, I know England was not plotting war." Of the *Lusitania* he said, "A terrible mistake." He listened eagerly to Miss Addams as she explained what the Peace Congress was urging, but at the end he shook his head; he could see no hope anywhere. And so we left him in his great, sombre library, a hopeless figure in deep mourning, stooping as he walked, torn continually with a racking cough, his cheeks and temples hollow, and his eyes sunken. We felt that he was in very truth a victim of the war, though he had never been in the trenches.

I can remember but two Germans who spoke to me with the sort of bitterness that I have heard from German-Americans over here, even though the war is so very close to them. I suspect that that is the real reason: that the tragedy is too great for rancor and uncharitableness. One woman said to me, when I quoted something from this side of the water: "I am far past all that now. At first I was bitter, but that is gone now. I have almost forgotten it." One must always remember that most Germans read nothing and hear nothing from the outside. I talked with an old friend, the wife of a professor under whom I worked years ago when I was studying bacteriology in Germany. She and her husband are people with cosmopolitan connections, they read three languages besides their own, and have always been as far removed as possible from narrow provincialism, but since last July they have known nothing except what their Government has decided that they shall know. I did not argue with my friend, but, of course, we talked much together and after she had been with us for three days she told me that she had never known before that there were people in England who did not wish to crush Germany, who wished for a just settlement, and even some who were opposed to the war.

Then she said: "I want you to believe this. We Germans think that the Fatherland was attacked without provocation, that our war is one of self-defence only. That is what we have been told. I begin to think it may not be true, but you must believe that we were sincere in our conviction."

In Berlin we had bread cards and we ate war bread. At each meal the waiter asked for our cards and snipped off one of the three coupons, then he brought us one and a half *Brödchen,* quite enough for breakfast and more than enough for the other meals. It was good bread—something like a cross between rye and white bread. They told us that this excessive economy was not really necessary, for as a matter of fact, Germany gets all the wheat she needs across the Russian border by bribing officials, but that the German Government wished to train the people in habits of saving. It has certainly been successful. I could not imagine being wasteful of bread in Berlin.

In Vienna, however, the bread cards seemed a real necessity, for the allowance of bread was very small, and as in Berlin, if one did not eat the three portions on a Monday, one could not save the coupon and get four on Tuesday. The slice given us three times a day was only two and a half inches long, two inches wide, and three-quarters of an inch thick, a pitifully small allowance for working people, to whom bread is the chief article of diet. It was a heavy, unappetizing bread, made of a mixture of potato flour, corn-meal, rye, and a very little wheat. The Viennese spoke with bitterness of the scarcity of wheat in Austria, saying that the Hungarians had plenty, but they were selling it to Prussia instead of to Austria.

In every country that we visited, people would ask us with pathetic eagerness if we did not find everything just the same as usual, if the city was not as gay as ever, life going on just the same, no sign of war anywhere. It would be a superficial person who could say that even of Berlin, and no one could say it of Vienna. We did not think that the people in Vienna had enough to eat; they looked, many of them, starved, more so than any people I have ever seen,—except, of course, in East London, where starvation seems endemic in normal times. I went one morning into the great *Stephanskirche.* No service was going on, but the church was full of people kneeling at every altar, one group of two hundred gathered together and chanting a litany quite without any leader, just by themselves. They were tragic-looking people, many of them the poorest of the poor. Among them were young recruits and wounded soldiers—the saddest congregation I have ever seen. Everywhere there are convalescent soldiers hobbling along the street, or wheeled in chairs, for the hospitals are scattered all over Vienna. The horses were so thin that one could count their ribs; we did not see one horse in decent condition while we were there. To add to the general impression of poverty, the walls and windows were covered with urgent appeals to the people to do their duty and subscribe to the second war loan.

We reached Vienna on the evening of Whitsunday. Italy had just declared war. That evening there was an attempt at a demonstration on the street under our balcony but it was not very warlike, just a crowd of young boys and girls singing the Austrian national hymn. The next day we passed a great troop of soldiers starting for the frontier. They were young fellows, almost all of them, some mere lads. They were very gay and proud and confident, and had bunches of flowers stuck in their belts and in their caps and even in the muzzles of their guns. That is really the most tragic thing one sees—the young men setting off gaily and confidently for the war. The wounded soldiers are bad enough, but at least they have come through alive.

In addition to seeing the minister of foreign affairs, and the prime minister of Austria—which was the real object of the visit to Vienna of course, we had also, as in Berlin, informal interviews with pacifists and others who were eager to hear what the committee had done and hoped to do. I remember meeting a very lovely woman who had gone to the Hague Congress simply because she felt that if in any country women were getting together to talk of peace, she must go and meet them. She was not a member of any woman's club and she had never spoken in public before, but she made one of the most moving speeches of the Congress. When I met her in Vienna, she told me that she had, since the first, been closely connected with the American Red Cross Hospital in Vienna, and that she had never heard a soldier speak with hatred or contempt of the men on the other side. That, she said, belonged to the non-fighters at home.

It was in Vienna that we heard the strongest protests against the censorship of the press. The meeting held there for the delegation was small and rather timid, yet it was a comfort to know that there was a group of women who had courage and broadmindedness enough to come together and ask to be told about the Peace Congress. Among our visitors was an old friend who is connected with shipping interests in Trieste and who was very indignant over the entrance of Italy into the war. He spoke of the unfounded claims of the Irredentists, saying that

though Trieste is predominantly Italian, the hinterland which it serves
is Slavic, and the Dalmatian coast has only a small minority of Italians.

There had been a question of our going to Budapest. Hungary has,
of course, no separate minister of foreign affairs, nor can she declare
war or peace independently of Austria. But Hungarians do not consider
themselves Austrians, and their present prime minister is generally said
to be the most influential man at present in the Empire Kingdom.
Moreover, the suffrage party in Budapest had endorsed the Peace Congress and the women were eager to have a large public meeting there.
Finally it was decided that the two Dutch ladies should go on to Berne
to attend a peace meeting there and that the two Americans should go
to Budapest.

Our short time there was crowded to overflowing. From the outset
it seemed to me quite different from either Berlin or Vienna and curiously like our own country, in spite of the Magyar which one heard everywhere. Our first breakfast seemed like home, because there was plenty
of bread and no bother about bread cards and before it was over a group
of journalists had arrived who were not only as eager for news as American journalists would be, but apparently as independent in their use of
it. We were quickly taken in charge by a group of very able women who
arranged for an interview with the prime minister and for a large public meeting. Miss Addams' speech was repeated in Magyar but I think
fully two-thirds of the audience understood English and were most re-
sponsive and sympathetic. When it was over, there was a dinner for
about sixty at the Ritz Hotel and it seemed characteristic of the spirit
of the country that a dignitary of the Roman Catholic Church, a pacifist
and also an outspoken feminist, should preside. There were members
of parliament and Government officials present, but the discussion at
the table was apparently as free and unconstrained as it would be in
America. The man who sat on my left was a privy councillor, who told
me frankly that he was a pacifist, that he had no use for Prussia, that he
considered that Hungary had no quarrel with Servia, certainly no desire to hurt Belgium, and that she was being forced to fight Prussia's war.
The woman on my right told me that she and her husband have put up
convalescent homes for some twelve hundred soldiers on their estate;
but she herself stays in Budapest and is chief cook, as she called it, for a
hospital with five hundred men. She has charge of all the supplies and

must plan the dietary so that she comes within the allowance made by the Government, yet she must give her soldiers enough nourishing food. If there is a deficit, it comes out of her pocket.

She told me that the English were generally liked in Hungary and that the people of Budapest are very proud of the fact that when the war broke out they had over five hundred English people in the city, and they have interned only about a dozen; the rest are all at liberty. We found also a very kindly feeling toward the Russians with whom, of course, the Hungarians have come in especially close contact. They say that fighting them is like fighting children, for the Russian peasant is averse to war and often has to be absolutely forced into it.

They told us the story of two Hungarians who had captured ten Russians, and one of the latter said, "Wait a minute and I will bring you some more." They let him go on the chance, thinking that anyway they had nine prisoners left, and presently he returned bringing with him thirty other Russians who willingly laid down their arms. They said, "We never wished to fight but now it is spring it is the season to till the soil; we will not fight any more; we wish to till the soil as we always do." So they have been put to work in the fields and are quite content.

In Budapest I was much impressed by my first experience of an official palace with many antechambers and men who, I felt sure, must be what historical novels call "lackeys." The prime minister looks curiously like pictures of General Grant, only that he is very tall and broad-shouldered. Like many Hungarians, he is a Presbyterian. He impresses one as a rather sombre, stern man with great resolution, but not as the fire-eater, the fierce war-lord, that the Austrians had described to us; certainly to us he said nothing of the glories or gains of war, only of its senseless horrors.

On our journey from Berne to Rome we stopped at Milan and at once were brought face to face with Italy in war paint, for the streets were decked with the flags of the five allies and placarded with posters reading "*Vogliamo Salandra.*" In the great arcade some of the shops had been wrecked by the mob. They told us that the city was at the time under martial law. The *Duomo* had been protected against possible Zeppelin raids by covering all the gilded portions of the roof with scaffolding and sandbags. It would never be difficult in Milan to stir up old animosity against the Austrians, but among the devices used to extend this to the

Germans we saw conspicuously displayed in the shop windows large photographs of a Belgian child with one hand cut off. This indubitable evidence of German atrocity was held second only to the fiery speeches of D'Annuncio as an aid in securing the proper war spirit among the Italians. It was evident from the photograph itself that the little hand had been carefully amputated, but such trifling evidence was of course not considered—and the old war story of mutilated children, utilized for hundreds of years in various countries, once more did its work.

Rome was at its loveliest, for the rains had kept a vivid spring green everywhere, but it was deserted as far as foreigners were concerned. Our hotel could serve us only our breakfast coffee and rolls, for cooks and waiters had been mobilized. Outwardly, the city was very gay. Constitution Day was celebrated while we were there, and the streets were filled with enormous crowds of holiday people and of soldiers in fresh uniforms, and flags were flying everywhere. The feeling seemed to be that the war could not possibly last long; now that Italy was in, it would soon be decided. Coming as we had from the sight of what nine months of war means to even so wonderfully organized a country as Germany, it filled us with dread to think what Rome would be like after a few months were over and she too had her cripples and her blinded men and widows and orphans and starving refugees.

It seemed little more than a formality to present the resolutions of the Peace Congress to ministers who had just triumphantly led Italy into war, but of course this was done. Afterwards we presented our letter from the Primate of Hungary to Cardinal Gasparri, secretary of state to the Pope, and through him secured an audience with the Pope himself. It was a real audience, for we sat for half an hour and discussed with him the war and the possibility of some action on the part of neutral nations to initiate negotiations between the warring countries. He was in favor of this, and said more than once that it was for the United States, the greatest of neutral countries, to make a move in which he would gladly coöperate if it seemed best.

We had had warning about the opposition the delegation would meet with in all of these countries, but especially had we been warned about France. It was true that though we found pacifists even in Paris, still the feeling there was on the whole more grimly determined, more immovable, than anywhere else. One can understand why this is so. France has been invaded, the richest part of her country is still in the hands of the conqueror, and her feeling is one of bitter resentment. It seemed to me also that we in America had never realized how universal has been the dread of just this disaster in the French mind. Over and over again I heard people say: "It does not matter what we have to endure if only we can at last free France from the nightmare of a German invasion."

No French woman had come to the Congress at The Hague, and a group of leading women had sent a protest against the holding of such a Congress. We had rather dreaded meeting in Paris even those women whom we knew, yet when we did meet a group of them, the delegation was able to make them see how the women at the Congress had felt and they on their side made us see that their bitterness was understandable, even if we could not share it. The war is terribly close to these women. Everyone I met that afternoon had at least one near and dear relative in danger at the front or already lost. They were all engaged in relief work of some kind, most of them spending their whole day at it, for that is the only thing that makes life bearable.

There is however a little band of pacifist women, most of them young, which has formed recently and is increasing all the time. There are also men in France who are willing to speak very frankly against prolonging the war to the bitter end. One of the members of the Chamber of Deputies introduced us to other like-minded members of the chamber, a goodly company. The news of Mr. Bryan's resignation had just come, and since the second note to Germany had not yet been published, everyone was feeling a bit apprehensive as to America's probable course of action. The deputies who talked to us all hoped that we would keep out of the war, for they said that the world needed a great neutral nation, not only to take charge of the embassies of the warring countries, to look after the welfare of prisoners of war, and to feed Belgium, but especially to help in the final settlement of the terms of peace.

In Paris, I had the impression even more strongly than elsewhere that the most extravagantly bitter statements are made, not by the Europeans themselves, but by the American sojourners in Europe. There is something very distasteful in this. It seems to me that no one has a right to urge extreme sacrifices unless he is also sacrificing himself, that nobody should talk of war to the bitter end who is not himself fighting. I remember how irritated I was by an American author, who lounged comfortably in the court of the hotel, smoking innumerable cigarettes, and nobly declaring his readiness to sacrifice the last Frenchmen in the trenches before he would yield an inch to Germany! Nor can I forget an American nurse who displayed with pride a ghoulish collection she had made of German and Austrian helmets, knapsacks, fragments of uniforms, bayonet ends, trophies of French battlefields, which she had bought from returned soldiers.

Of the ministers whom the delegation interviewed in Paris, the minister of foreign affairs, a life-long militarist, was less approachable than most of the ministers whom the delegations met, although the president of the *Conseil* who performs the offices of a prime minister was much more moderate than he.

The informal interviews were sometimes depressing, sometimes quite inspiring. Perhaps the most depressing were those with former pacifists, who in bitter disillusionment over the failure of their hopes and in mortification over the ridicule they had received, had become almost more militaristic than the military.

Poor little Belgium has had to accept the hospitality of France and her Government is housed in hotels and villas on the seashore near Havre. The Belgian minister for foreign affairs was a sad, gentle person, who took the mission of the delegation very seriously and spoke with real feeling of Belgium's longing for peace, although, as he said, she was in the hands of her allies and must leave such things to them.

With this visit the work of the delegation was over until the resolutions could be presented to Washington. As, however, we were to sail from Liverpool, we had a week to spend in London, and put it to very good use. London seemed to me more changed by the war than any city except Vienna, partly because the sight of soldiers in London is unusual, and because what seemed natural in Berlin was unnatural there. Then, too, there are posters covering every available space and appealing to all possible motives which might induce men to join the army.

It was a relief to reach a country where speech is free and where critics of the Government can make themselves heard in Hyde Park, or in pamphlets such as those issued by the Union for Democratic Control. Our days were filled with meetings, formal and informal, interviews arranged by the very capable British committee. We met in England a large number of men and women who recognized England's responsibility in the remoter causes of the war and who are determined to do their utmost to bring about a permanent peace on the basis of justice and human needs rather than on that of political ambitions. To many of these even the invasion of Belgium did not justify a return to the outworn ways of violence. Some of these, as one would expect, were Quakers who seemed to us to be playing a very fine part just now in England. They have remained surprisingly faithful to their principles and while serving their country in ways which expose them to great danger, they will do only those things that tend to preserve life not to destroy it. We dined with a Quaker family the three children of which had gone to the war. The eldest son is doing ambulance work in Flanders, carrying the wounded from the battlefield to the base hospital, than which no work is more perilous; the second son is engaged in sweeping mines in the North Sea; and his sister nurses in a hospital in Dunkirk, which has repeatedly been shelled.

Oxford was very sad, but we were told that during term time the contrast with the Oxford one used to know was even greater. As we walked through the colleges, our hosts would point out the new kind of honor list hanging on the wall of chapel or cloister, the list of students who have already fallen in the war, and they would tell us of this one or that, of his great promise or his charming qualities, so that the names took on a reality even to us. As I remember it, St. John's has been converted into a school for refugee Belgian boys, Balliol was filled with the officers of the training camps, other colleges with young recruits. Then there are the big hospitals under Sir William Osler, one of them devoted entirely to men who have breathed the poisonous gases and yet survived.

In England, more than in any country, we heard of doubts and questionings on the part of the young men, especially those from the universities, who cannot reconcile the thought of killing other men with what they have always held as their ideal of conduct, and yet who cannot refuse to respond to their country's call.

It is hard to sum up general impressions from this journey, there are so many of them. One, however, I should like to speak of, for it is borne in upon me so strongly now that I am at home again. That is, that there is in the countries mutually at war no such universal desire to fight on to the bitter end as we suppose over here. We judge largely by the newspapers which come to us from that side and which are of course strictly censored.

I find that people here are often indignant, if not actually resentful, at the mere suggestion that negotiations be substituted for force at the earliest possible moment. They seem to be much impressed with the things that must be gained by war before war can be allowed to stop, but I believe this means that they do not realize what war has already cost the countries engaged in it and what more it will cost if it is to continue. The men at the head of affairs over there are not blind and they do realize it, and so do many thinking people in every country, and so would Americans if they could see for themselves and were not obliged to form their judgment simply on what the warring Governments allow the newspapers to say. Those nations are committing race suicide and impoverishing their children and grandchildren, and they know it, yet they seem to be unable to find any way to end it.

They do not need us to encourage them to keep on, but it may be that they need us to help them to find a way out.

3

The Revolt against War

(a) By Certain Young Men
(b) By Groups of Civilians

JANE ADDAMS

🖎 The details of our visits to the various war capitals are given in the official report of the Congress and for obvious reasons are omitted from this narrative account. It would also be most unwise to repeat our experiences with any one Government, but certain impressions received in all of the capitals so unmistakably have to do with war as an institution and with its reactions on the civil population that no confidence can be violated in stating them although it is most difficult to formulate our experience, brought face to face as we were with so much genuine emotion and high patriotism as is exhibited in the warring nations of Europe at the present moment. We became very much afraid of generalizing; the situation is so complicated and so many wild statements are made in regard to it that it is farthest from our purpose to add to this already overwhelming confusion, or to "let loose" any more emotion upon the world. We came to feel that what is needed above all else is some human interpretation of this overevolved and much-talked-of situation in which so much of the world finds itself in dire confusion and bloodshed. In regard to such generalizations as we do venture to make, it is necessary to guard against one or two possible misapprehensions. The delegations from the Congress at The Hague visited the ministry of each nation, who of course represent the civil aspect of government as it is carried on year after year when there is no war. In every country, we were received by a committee of women connected officially with the Congress at The Hague, who had arranged that we should speak in public to larger or smaller audiences, and in every country we naturally met the friends of these women, the mothers of men who were at the front, nurses in the hospitals, and many others. We saw Socialists, aghast at the violence resulting to their international views from the war but already beginning to recover from the first impact; groups of Christians or Jews whose conceptions of religious solidarity had been outraged. We came in touch with new types of pacifist organizations, thrown up by the war, taking the place of the old pacifists, who with few exceptions were submerged by the flood-tide of militarism.

I came to believe that there must be many more of the same type in every country, quite as eager for the retention and development of their national ideals and quite as patriotic as the militarists, but believing with all their hearts that militarism cannot establish those causes which are most dear to them, that human nature has been forced into unnatural channels by the war and that their children are being sacrificed for a purpose which can never be obtained through warfare. I do not wish to imply that in any country we found open division between the people. On the contrary we found that the war had united men, women, and children in a common cause and had bound them together in an overwhelming national consciousness.

Our first striking experience was to find that the same causes and reasons for the war were heard everywhere. Each belligerent nation solemnly assured us that it was fighting under the impulse of self-defence, to preserve its traditions and ideals from those who would come in to disturb and destroy them. And in every capital we heard the identical phrases describing the good qualities of the citizens within the country, and very much the same derogatory phrases in regard to the enemy whom they were fighting. On one point only they always differed and that was in regard to the responsibility for the war.

We always found some officials ready to indict the entire situation. I have never heard war indicted with more earnestness than by responsible men in the belligerent nations. Of course they all deprecated the loss of the youth upon whom depended the progress of the nation and the tremendous debts fastened upon the backs of the humble people. On the other hand, they were all of the opinion that this war was inevitable, and in the end would make for progress.

The warring nations presented another point of similarity; from many people whom we met in each of them we were forced to infer that a certain type of young man did not want the war and considered the older men responsible for it, that enthusiasm for the war was not as universal among the young men who were doing the fighting as it was among the elderly men established in the high places of church and state; that it was the older men who had convinced themselves that this was a righteous war which must be fought to a finish; that there were to be found in each nation young men in the trenches convinced that war was not a legitimate method of settling international difficulties.

Doubtless this is but a partial view. I am quite sure that the large majority of young men in the trenches are confident that they are performing the highest possible duty; that the spirit of righteousness is in the hearts of most of them, but I am also convinced that there are to be found these other men who are doing violence to the highest teachings which they know.

It seemed to me at moments as if the difference between the older generation and the new is something we apprehend dimly in each country; that the older men believed more in abstractions; that certain theological or nationalistic words, patriotic phrases included, meant more to them than they did to young men who had come to take life as it was revealed through experience, who were more pragmatic in their philosophy, who more empirical in their point of view.

Certain young men in England contended that the older men, surviving as a product of the Victorian age, responded to slogans which had not the same meaning in the ears of this generation; that an intense narrow patriotism was one of them; that the older men were nearer to the type that had been ready to fight for religious abstraction, nearer to the age when men lined up in opposing forces to fight out a difference in dogma as to the composition of the Trinity; and that the governmentalists have reared new abstractions. It is this feeling that causes the protest among the young men, who are still asking new experiences, new contacts with other nations, new reactions to the intelligence of other hemispheres. These young men at the outbreak of the war were just beginning to make themselves felt, they were responding to the promptings toward a new order which might in the end have done away with standing armies and camps. At the present moment they feel themselves violently thrown back and bidden play a role in a drama of life which they were outgrowing. Such young men have no notion of shirking their duty, of not standing up to the war at their country's demand, but they go into the trenches with a divided mind which is tragic. Tragedy after all is not a conflict between good and evil; tragedy from the time of Aeschylus has been the conflict between one good and another, between two kinds of good, so that the mind of the victim is torn as to which he ought to follow, which should possess his entire allegiance. That sort of tragedy, I am sure, is in the minds of certain young men who are fighting upon every side of the great conflict.

Even in their conception of internationalism, the two groups of young men and old men differed widely. The Victorian group, for instance, in their moral romanticism, fostered a sentiment for a far-off "Federation of the World," and believed that the world would be federated when wise men from many nations met together and accomplished it. The young men do not talk much about internationalism, but they live in a world where common experience has in fact become largely internationalized. A young Frenchman, employed in the Parisian office of a large business enterprise, told me that the day war was declared he went out of the door with an Englishman and a German with whom he had been associated for four years. The three men shook hands in front of the locked door and each man went to fight for his country, but the two said to the third: "We hope never to be brought up against you in the line of battle." They had no theory about loving each other, but in point of fact a genuine friendship had transcended national bounds. The men of the older generation have not shared so largely in such experiences which the new internationalism implies, nor in their devotion to abstract ideas are they so open to modification through experience.

The young men therefore, when bidden to go to war on a purely national issue, have a tendency to question whether that which they are doing is useful and justifiable and are inclined to more or less test it out. Such testing is indeed in line with their philosophy, for while empirically grounded truths do not inspire such violent loyalty as *a priori* truths, they "are more discussable and have a human and social quality," we are told.

This notion that the old gulf between fathers and sons is once more yawning wide in Europe may be a superficial one, but I am at least recording the impression we received in one country after the other.

Doubtless at the beginning of the war, the young men even more en-thusiastically than the old were caught up into that consciousness of a strong and united nation which has carried its citizens to heights of self-sacrifice which human nature seldom attains, and they all responded to that primitive ethic founded upon obedience to group sentiment and the need of race safety which so completely asserted its sway over that more highly developed ethic supposed to be the possession of the civ-ilized world. But just as there is a gradual return on the part of the Socialists, for instance, to those doctrines of internationalism and peace which they have preached for half a century, so thousands of other cit-izens are going back to the moral positions they held before the war. The young are perhaps the most eager to make clear their changing position; they continue to salute the flag, but recognize it as a symbol and realize that it has the danger of all abstractions, that a wrong con-tent may be substituted for the right one, and that men in a nation, an army, a crowd may do things horrible as well as heroic that they could never do alone.

The older men have no conception of the extent to which the purely nationalistic appeal has been weakened. They themselves say that this war with its sturdy nationalistic ideals and ambitions shows what non-sense all the talk of internationalism has been and how absurd were the Hague Conferences, although in the very same speech I heard an En-glishman say also that Great Britain went into war to protest against the illegal and unjustifiable invasion of Belgium because solemn inter-national treaties had been broken, admitting that international obli-gations are so genuine that blood must be spilled to preserve them.

The young men on the contrary speak with no uncertain sound. We met one young German who said: "I happen to live near the line of Schleswig-Holstein. I am told the men of Schleswig-Holstein are my brothers, but my grandfather before me fought them. I do not know whether they are my brothers or my grandfather's enemies; I only know I have no feeling for them different from that I have for men living far-ther north in Denmark itself. The truth is that neither to my grandfa-ther nor to me do the people of Schleswig-Holstein mean anything; that he hated them and that I love them are both fictions, invented and fos-tered for their own purposes by the people who have an interest in war." The man who said this was a fine young fellow who had been wounded and sent home to be cured; in those solemn days he was trying to think the thing out and he asked himself what it was he was doing with this life of his. What impresses one in regard to these young men is that it is so desperately irrevocable, that it is their very lives which are demanded. The older men who have had honor and fullness of life and have been put into high places in the state, who are they to deprive even one of these young men of that which should lie before him?

It is obviously quite impossible to know how many young men there are in a similar state of mind, how many more mothers like the one who said to us: "It was hard to see my boy go because he did not believe in war; he did not belong to a generation that believes in war."

One of the leading men of Europe is authority for the statement: "If this war could have been postponed for ten years,—perhaps," he said, "I will be safe and say, twenty years,—war would have been impossible in Europe, because of the tremendous revolt against it in the schools and the universities."

Certainly we found such revolt in England, to quote from a letter published in the *Cam-Magazine* at Cambridge University and written by a young man who had gone to the front, joining that large number of students who have almost depleted the universities.

> "The greatest trial that this war has brought is that it has released the old men from all restraining influences, and has let them loose upon the world. The city editors, the retired majors, the amazons, and last, but I fear, not least, the venerable archdeacons, have never been so free from contradiction. Just when the younger generation was beginning to take its share in the affairs of the world, and was hoping to counteract the Victorian influences of the older generation, this war has come to silence us,—permanently or temporarily as the case may be. Meanwhile, the old men are having field days on their own. In our name, and for our sakes, as they pathetically imagine, they are doing their very utmost, it would seem, to perpetuate, by their appeals to hate, intolerance, and revenge, those very follies which have produced the present conflagration."

A professor in an English university showed us a letter written in a military hospital by one of his students, in which the young man congratulated himself upon the loss of a leg because it enabled him to resume reasonable living with an undivided mind. He had responded to his country's call in deference to the opinion of older men. He would now return to the ideas of his own generation.

A letter from one of those young ardent spirits fighting in the opposing trenches written to his fiancée runs as follows:

> "I rouse my indignation and awaken all my powers to put my thoughts in order, that, should I return from this war, I might fling them once for all in the faces of men who deceive themselves into finding a justification for all this murdering; and who further believe—Heaven knows why—that there will be great moral effects from this wholesale slaughter. As if civilized men were ever justified for any principle whatever, to suddenly fall into the madness of letting loose on one another with instruments of murder."

It gradually became clear to us that whether it is easily recognized or not, there has grown up a generation in Europe, as there has doubtless grown up a generation in America, who have revolted against war. It is a god they know not of, whom they are not willing to serve; because all of their sensibilities and their training upon which their highest ideals depend, revolt against it.

We met a young man in Switzerland who had been in the trenches for three months and had been wounded there. He did not know that he had developed tuberculosis but he thought he was being cured, and he was speaking his mind before he went back to the trenches. He was, I suppose, what one would call a fine young man, but not an exceptional one. He had been in business with his father and had travelled in South Africa, in France, England, and Holland. He had come to know men as *Mensch,* that *gute Menschen* were to be found in every land. And now here he was, at twenty-eight, facing death because he was quite sure when he went back to the trenches that death awaited him. He said that never during that three months and a half had he once shot his gun in a way that could possibly hit another man and nothing in the world could make him kill another man. He could be ordered into the trenches and "to go through the motions," but the final act was in his own hands and with his own conscience. And he said: "*My* brother is an officer." He gave the name and rank of his brother, for he was quite too near the issues of life and death for any shifting and concealing. "He never shoots in a way that will kill. And I know dozens and dozens of young men who do not."

We talked with nurses in hospitals, with convalescent soldiers, with mothers of those who had been at home on furlough and had gone back into the trenches, and we learned that there are surprising numbers of young men who will not do any fatal shooting because they think that no one has the right to command them to take human life. From one hospital we heard of five soldiers who had been cured and were ready to be sent back to the trenches, when they committed suicide, not because they were afraid to die but they would not be put into a position where they would have to kill others.

I recall a spirited young man who said: "We are told that we are fighting for civilization but I tell you that war destroys civilization. The highest product of the universities, the scholar, the philosopher, the poet, when he is in the trenches, when he spends his days and nights in squalor and brutality and horror, is as low and brutal as the rudest peasant. They say, those newspaper writers, that it is wonderful to see the courage of the men in the trenches, singing, joking, playing cards, while the shells fall around them. Courage there is no room for, just as there is no room for cowardice. One cannot rush to meet the enemy, one cannot even see him. The shells fall here or they fall there. If you are brave, you cannot defy them; if you are a coward, you cannot flee from them; it is all chance. You see the man you were playing cards with a while ago lying on the ground a bloody mass and you look at him and think, 'Well, this time it took him; in a few minutes it may be my turn; let's go back to the cards.' And all the time you loathe the squalor, the brutality, the savages around you, and the savage you are yourself becoming. Why should you kill men who live in other countries, men whom in times of peace you would like and respect? At least I can say that as yet I have escaped the horror of killing anyone."

It is such a state of mind which is responsible for the high percentage of insanity among the soldiers. In the trains for the wounded there is often a closed van in which are kept the men who have lost their minds. Sometimes they recover after due care, and sometimes they prove to be hopelessly insane. A young Russian wrote home: "Men have fought from the beginning of history, yet no one has ever recorded that so many soldiers lost their minds, were driven mad by war. Do you suppose it was true always, or is it only true in this generation?"

In every country we heard of the loathing against the use of the bayonet felt by this type of young man to whom primitive warfare was especially abhorrent, although he was a brave soldier and serving his country with all his heart. We heard from interned soldiers in Holland that they had escaped across the border dazed and crazed after a bayonet charge; from hospital nurses who said that delirious soldiers are again and again possessed by the same hallucination—that they are in the act of pulling their bayonets out of the bodies of men they have killed; from the returned soldiers one of whom said to us: "A bayonet charge does not show courage, but madness. Men must be brought to the point by stimulants and once the charge is begun they are like insane men. I have been in it and after it was over I was utterly dazed. I did not know what had happened to me any more than if I had been picked up from the water after an explosion on shipboard."

We were told in several countries that in order to inhibit the sensibilities of this type of man, stimulants were given to the soldiers before a charge was ordered; that the giving of stimulants was a quicker process than that incitement to reprisals and revenge which in actual warfare often serves as an immediate incentive. In illustration of such substitution, a Frenchman said that "since the use of poisonous gases by the Germans, no further stimulants would be needed for a thoroughly indignant and aroused soldiery"; an Englishman spoke of the difficulties in the early months of the war in overcoming the *camaraderie* unhappily evinced by certain British troops for the Saxons long established in an opposite trench, and the relief when the Bavarians took their places, against whom no incitement to hostility was necessary.

It never occurred to us who heard this statement, nor to those who made it, that this was done because the men lacked courage. It would be impossible of course from one type of man to make any generalizations in regard to the "average" soldier. One of the hideous results of war is the inveterate tendency of the "average" man to fall into the spirit of retaliation. We were told in two countries that the soldiers were being supplied as fast as possible with short knives because they could not advantageously use their bayonets in the occasional hand-to-hand encounters within the trenches themselves and we, of course, know of the men who said of the bayonet charge: "Ah, that is fighting, when the primitive man lets himself go and does the sort of fighting which is personal and definite!" We heard tales of the reactions on both types of men and it is farthest from my intention to add one word to the campaign of calumny, to disparage either the motives or the courage of the long line of fighting soldiers, to repeat one tale of horror which might increase that poverty of heart induced by hatred.

In addition to the revolt against war on the part of the young men, there was discernible everywhere among the civilian population two bodies of enthusiasm: one, and by far the larger, believes that the war can be settled only upon a military basis after a series of smashing victories; the other, a civil party, very much deprecates the exaltation of militarism and contends that the longer the war is carried on, the longer the military continues censoring the press and exercising other powers not ordinarily accorded to it—thus breaking down safeguards of civil government, many of which have been won at the hardest—the more difficult it will be for normal civil life to reëstablish itself.

Many of the people whom we met were therefore anxious that the war should be speedily terminated—of course always a peace with honor—if only because of its effect upon the internal development of national life. They believed in the war and yet they labored under a certain apprehension that the longer it was continued the more difficult it would be for the civil authorities to win back the liberties they had once possessed. In the warring capitals, citizens are under military law and are subject to fine and imprisonment, or both, for its infraction. The military authorities can, on mere suspicion, arrest a citizen without warrant and also enter his house. Such "defence of the realm" acts are submitted too patiently as a part of war, but the people who represent the civil view of life, even in the midst of their patriotic fervor and devotion to the army, long for some other form of settlement than that obtained by military victory. While they ardently desire a release from the intolerable strain, they realize that to have salvation come through the army would be to desperately entrench militarism and to add dangerously to its prestige and glory.

In Germany we met patriotic citizens who felt that one of the dangers of a peace determined through military successes, especially if those were won on the eastern front, would be the likelihood that terms would be made through Russia, establishing militarism yet more firmly. If peace were made through negotiations, then the western nations under England's lead would have the preponderance of influence; that is, the military authorities would be more sympathetic to the Russian type of settlement and the civil authorities to the western type. The longer the war goes on, however, the more likely it is that the settlement will depend upon the victories of one nation or the other.

We were told in England that this war in essence is a conflict between militarism and democracy, but the situation is obviously not so simple as that. War itself destroys democracy wherever it thrives and tends to entrench militarism. If the object of the war is to down militarism, it must be clear that the very prolongation of the war entrenches the military ideal not only in Russia and Germany, but in the more democratic nations as well. No one would urge that a settlement through negotiations is the only way to preserve democratic institutions, but certainly the present method runs great risk. The immediacy of negotiations is therefore a factor in the situation. They should be begun while the civil authorities still have enough power to hold the military to their own purposes and are not obliged to give them the absolute control of the destinies of the nation. If you point out to an Englishman that democracy will not gain if German militarism is crushed and a new war party sits in every capital of Europe, he will tell you that such a situation, if it arises, must be attended to afterwards, that at present the allies are crushing the Prussian type of militarism. It seems clear however to the neutral observer that in the meantime, while the crushing process goes on, militarism is firmly lodged in men's minds and that no body of men is seriously trying to discover how far militarism is being crushed by this war or how far civil forces are merely becoming exhausted and methods of negotiation discredited.

The belief that the restitution of Belgium can only be obtained through "driving out the invaders" by an opposing army has already become established in the minds of thousands of people. Yet we met, during our weeks in Europe, many exiled Belgians, who told us they could not go back to their own country because of the fear that the Germans would be beaten back over the same territory that had already been devastated and that a retreating army is always the worst. Some of these Belgians hoped that Belgium would be evacuated through negotiations and treaties, and yet so completely has method become confused with aim in this war, militarism with the object to be accomplished, that in the desire to drive the invaders out, the aim of getting

the peaceful Belgians back in their own country was for the moment
overshadowed, although to accomplish this through negotiation rather
than bloodshed would be an enormous gain for all concerned. There
are civilians in Germany who are anxious to hold the German gener-
als to their own statement that they marched through Belgium as a
matter of military necessity and not for conquest, and early in July a
petition, signed by eighty-four leading men of Germany, was presented to the Chancellor, urging that there be no annexation of territory
as a result of the war.

If the Germans are to evacuate Belgium without bloodshed, it must
be through the coöperation of such groups of civilians as these. It is the
civilian who is interested in freeing the channels of trade, in breaking
down unnatural tariff walls, and restoring life to a normal basis.

Yet so long as the military process absorbs the attention of all of
Europe, it is obvious that groups of civilians in different countries are
constantly becoming so enfeebled that their counsels may easily be
overborne.

Everywhere we were conscious of a certain revolt, not of nationalistic feeling nor of patriotism, but of human nature itself as of hedged
in, harassed peoples, "as if the Atlantic Ocean had been partitioned with
great bulkheads into private seas and the Gulf Stream blocked in its
course." There had apparently been an accumulation within national
borders of those higher human affections which should have had an
outlet into the larger life of the world but could not, because no international devices had been provided for such expression. No great central authority had been dealing with this sum of human goodwill, as a
scientist deals with the body of knowledge in his subject irrespective
of its national origins, and the nations themselves became confused
between what was legitimate patriotism and those universal emotions
which have nothing to do with national frontiers.

4

Factors in Continuing the War

(a) The Press
(b) Isolation of Peace Advocates
(c) No Adequate Offer of Negotiations

JANE ADDAMS

✍ Travelling rapidly, as we did, from one country to another, perhaps nothing was more striking than the diametrically opposing opinions we found concerning identical occurrences or series of events.

We arrived in London two days after the sinking of the *Lusitania* and read in many columns the indignation against this "crowning outrage of German piracy upon helpless women and children." So profound was this feeling that during the next few days when we were still in London, the English Parliament, following the attacks upon the German bakeshops and other places of business, decided to intern German subjects. Ten days later when we reached Berlin, their citizens were still rejoicing over the victory which had been achieved by a tiny submarine over the "great auxiliary cruiser of the British Navy," in phrases reminding us of the old story in our school books about the *Monitor* and the *Merrimac.*

Inevitably the inferences from these widely divergent facts were irreconcilable. Even reasonable and justice-loving people in both countries, who wished to be sure of their data before passing judgment, would be quite unable to deal impartially with the situation. As to the large number of people found on both sides who grasp eagerly at any atrocity which may justify or increase the bitter animosity against the enemy, we were absolutely unable to determine whether the hate produced the atrocities, or the atrocities the hate.

Almost every tale we heard in London of outrages on the part of German soldiers against the helpless Belgians was repeated in Vienna of the brutal behavior of the Cossack soldiers in East Prussia. Our delegation reached Italy ten days after war was declared against Austria.

A Socialist Member of Parliament, proud of the fact that his party had voted against the war appropriation, told us unequivocally that "This was a newspaper-made war,"—that a campaign conducted throughout the winter had culminated in a sensational three days, when the people reached the highest degree of excitement. One is, of course, reminded of the old nursery riddle: Which is first, the egg or the hen? Does public opinion control the press or the reverse? It was perhaps inevitable for our Socialist friend to believe that the great Italian banks with their interests in Dalmatia were the actual power.

The press everywhere tended to make an entire nation responsible for the crimes of individuals, a tendency which is certainly fraught with awful consequences, even though the crimes for which the nation is held responsible may have originated in the gross exaggeration of some trivial incident. The very size and extent of the contention acts like a madness.

This perhaps accounts for the impression left upon our minds that in the various countries the enthusiasm for continuing the war is fed largely on a fund of animosity growing out of the conduct of the war. Germany is indignant because England's blockade was an attempt to starve her women and children; England is on fire over the German atrocities in Belgium. A young man in France said, "We hope to be able very soon to squirt petroleum into the German trenches so that everything will easily catch fire." I replied, "That seems very terrible." "Yes," he said, "but think of the poisonous gas and the horrible death of our men who were asphyxiated."

In each country, we were told of hideous occurrences of warfare which demonstrated that the continued existence of the enemy was a menace to civilization. Constantly one hears that Germany has done this; the allies have done that; somebody tried to do this and we prevented it by doing that. But after all, great nations, however legitimate the first cause of war may have been, cannot conduct their operations from the standpoint of reprisals, which is not a permissible method even among small groups. Occasionally we met a man who said, "Of course, in the end the war must be adjudicated with the original causes as a factor, but we are getting farther away from the causes every day, and more and more the conduct of the war is modifying its aim."

Is it because this war has been carried to the very doorsteps of those people in Europe who have reached a stage of sensibility towards human suffering and an understanding of the differing individual which has never been obtained before in human history, that the gathering horror drives them on? Or is the mind of Europe submerged under a great emotionalism, inhibiting normal family affections and daily interests so that thousands of people joyfully surrender their children and all their possessions. A Frenchman looking around his library said to us: "I used to think there was something valuable in these books, but I would throw them at once into the trenches, if their burning would so heat the hands of a soldier that he might shoot to kill one man of that nation which is destroying the liberties of Europe."

Nevertheless the fanatical patriotism which has risen so high in these countries, and which is essentially so fine and imposing, cannot last. The wave will come down, the crest cannot be held indefinitely. Then men must see the horrible things which are taking place not as causes for continuing the war, but as that which must never be allowed to occur again. At the present moment, however, the man whose burning heart can find no slightest justification for the loss of the finest youth of Europe unless it results in the establishment of such international courts as will make war forever impossible, finds it difficult to discover a vehicle through which he may express this view. International ideals for the moment are treated not only with derision and contempt but as dangerous to patriotism.

In every country we found evidence of a group of men and women—how large, we were, of course, unable to determine—who although they were not opposed to the war and regarded their own countries as sinned against and not as sinning, still felt that their respective countries ought to be content with a limited programme of victory. Yet even in England a man who says that peace ought to be made with Germany on any other terms than dictation by the allies is attacked by the newspapers as pro-German, without any reference as to whether those terms are favorable or not to his country.

A good patriot of differing opinion finds it almost impossible to reach his fellow countrymen with that opinion, because he would not for the world print anything which might confuse the popular mind, for war belongs to that state of society in which right and wrong must be absolute.

The huge agglomerations of human beings of which modem society is composed communicate with each other largely through the printed word and, poor method as it is, apparently public opinion cannot be quickly discovered through any other agency. Certainly the most touching interview we had on the continent was with a man who had been in a responsible position in England when war was declared and who was over-burdened equally with the sense that he had failed to convince his countrymen that the war was unnecessary and with the futility of making any further effort.

This lack of mobilization of public opinion in so many of the countries of Europe is at present a serious aspect of the war. Even in the most autocratic countries, Governments respond to public opinion and governmental policies are modified as men of similar opinion gather into small groups, as they make a clear statement of that opinion, and as they promote larger groups. At the present moment this entire process in the modification of governmental policies is brought to a standstill among the warring nations, even in England where the very method of governmental change depends upon the registry of public opinion.

But as like-minded people within the borders of a warring nation cannot find each other, much less easily can the search be conducted beyond the lines of battle. As we went from one country to another, people would say, "Did you find anyone taking our line, thinking as we do?" The people, as a whole, do not know even the contemplated terms of settlement and could only learn them through a free and courageous press, while the governmental officials themselves could only thus obtain a full knowledge of public opinion concerning the continuance of the war. Every public man in Europe knows that before the rulers will think of peace, they must know that behind them, if they advocate peace, there would be a grateful and passionate opinion ready to support them against the militarists. Even pacifically inclined ministers in the Government itself dare not talk of treating with the enemy while the only vocal opinion in newspapers and speeches is in favor of fighting till the enemy surrenders unconditionally. Preëminently in Great Britain and Germany any peace negotiation can be stopped by the militarist elements, which predominate during war in Government circles. But how can peace processes be begun if none of the leading journals dare call upon "the various Governments to declare what to each nation is the essential and indispensable condition for ceasing the conflict," which would of course be but a preliminary to negotiations and the final terms of peace. If in the end adjustment must be reached through the coming together of like-minded people in the contending nations, it is a thousand pities that it should fail through lack of a mechanism whereby they might find each other. In the meantime, the very foundations of a noble national life are being everywhere undermined by the constant disparagement of other nations, and as each fears nothing more than an appearance of the weariness of the war, the desire for peace filling many hearts is denied all journalistic expression while the war spirit is continually fed by the outrages of the war, as flames are fed by fuel.

At moments I found myself filled with a conviction that the next revolution against tyranny would have to be a revolution against the unscrupulous power of the press. A distinguished European, accustomed to addressing the civilized world through the printed page, finding himself unable to reach even his own countrymen, suggested to us the plight of a caged lion as he vehemently walked up and down a little alcove in our hotel, expressing his exasperation and despair. To my mind the message he was not permitted to give was the one which Europe needed above all others and the self-exiled pacifists, French, German, Austrian, English, and Belgian, whom we met in Switzerland, were a curious comment on the freedom of the press.

Two conclusions were inevitably forced upon us. First: that the people of the different countries could not secure the material upon which they might form a sound judgment of the situation, because the press with the opportunity of determining opinion by selecting data, had assumed the power once exercised by the church when it gave to the people only such knowledge as it deemed fit for them to have. Second: that in each country the leading minds were not bent upon a solution nor to the great task that would bring international order out of the present anarchy, because they were absorbed in preconceived judgments, and had become confused through the limitations imposed upon their sources of information. The civilian point of view and even a hint of the revolt against war was reflected in the foreign offices themselves as we visited one after another in five weeks. We were received by Prime Minister Cort van der Linden and Foreign Minister Loudon, in The Hague; Prime Minister Asquith and Foreign Minister Sir Edward Grey, in London; Reichskanzler von Bethmann-Hollweg and Foreign Minister von Jagow, in Berlin; Prime Minister Stuergkh and Foreign Minister Burian, in Vienna; Prime Minister Tisza, in Budapest; Prime Minister Salandra and Foreign Minister Sonino, in Rome; Prime Minister Viviani and Foreign Minister Delcassé, in Paris; Foreign Minister d'Avignon, in Havre; President Motta and Foreign Minister Hoffman, in Berne.

Our message was a simple one. After discussing our resolutions we ventured to report to the men who are after all responsible for the happenings of Europe that the fifteen hundred women who met in The Hague, coming in smaller or larger numbers from twelve different countries, urge that whatever the causes of the war and however necessary it may have been to carry it on for the past ten months, that the time has come for beginning some sort of negotiations which must in the end take place unless the war shall continue year after year and at last be terminated through sheer exhaustion. We implied that if Europe is in disorder because of deep-rooted injustices or because certain nations are deprived of commercial, political, or maritime opportunities, than the solution can be discovered much better by men who consider the situation on its merits than by those who approach it on the basis of military victories or losses.

In reply to this we heard everywhere, again in very similar phrases, that a nation at war cannot ask for negotiations nor even express a willingness for them, lest the enemy at once construe it as a symptom of weakness, for when the terms are made, the side which first suggested negotiations will suffer as being considered the weaker side suing for peace.

But they said, in all save one of these foreign offices, that tentative propositions should first be presented by some outside power,—if neutral people commanding the respect of the foreign offices to whom their propositions would be presented should study the situation seriously and make propositions, over and over again if necessary, something might be found upon which negotiations might begin, and that there were none of the warring nations that would not be ready to receive such service.

It may be natural for the minister of a nation at war to say, "This country will never receive negotiations; we are going to drive the enemy out inch by inch," but it is difficult for him to repeat it to a delegation of women who reply: "If a feasible proposition were presented to you, which might mean the beginning of negotiations between your country and your enemies, would you decline to receive such a proposition? Would you feel justified to go on sacrificing the young men of your country in order to attain through bloodshed what might be obtained by negotiations, the very purpose for which the foreign office was established?" No minister, of course, is willing to commit himself to such an undeviating policy.

On the contrary one of them said that he had wondered many times since the war began why women had remained silent so long, adding that as women are not expected to fight they might easily have made a protest against war which is denied to men.

We went into the office of another high official, a large, grizzled, formidable man. When we had finished our presentation and he said nothing, I remarked, "It perhaps seems to you very foolish that women should go about in this way; but after all, the world itself is so strange in this war situation that our mission may be no more strange nor foolish than the rest."

He banged his fist on the table. "Foolish?" he said. "Not at all. These are the first sensible words that have been uttered in this room for ten months."

He continued: "That door opens from time to time, and people come in to say, 'Mr. Minister, we must have more men, we must have more ammunition, we must have more money or we cannot go on with this war.' At last the door opens and two people walk in and say, 'Mr. Minister, why not substitute negotiations for fighting?' They are the sensible ones."

Other people, of course, said that he was an old man and losing his political power. Yet he was an officer of the Government in high place and the incident is repeated for whatever value it may have. It is by no means an isolated one, and we had other testimonials of the same sort from the people whose nations are at war.

Our mission was simple, and foolish it may be, but it was not impossible. Perhaps the ministers talked freely to us because we were so absolutely unofficial. "Without abandoning your cause and without lowering your patriotism," we practically said to the representatives of these various nations, "whatever it is which you ought in honor to obtain, why are you not willing to submit your case to a tribunal of fair-minded men? If your cause is as good as you are sure it is, certainly such men will find the righteousness which adheres within it." Responsible people in all the warring powers said that if the right medium could be found, there would be no difficulty in submitting the case.

We do not wish to overestimate a very slight achievement nor to take too seriously the kindness with which the delegation was received, but we do wish to record ourselves as being quite sure that at least a few citizens in these various countries, some of them officials in high places, were grateful for the effort we made.

5

At the Northern Capitals

EMILY G. BALCH

✍ The second delegation, of which I was a member, was assigned to the Scandinavian countries and to Russia.

The delegation was made up of one from each of the belligerent sides and one from two neutral countries. It comprised Chrystal Macmillan, one of the two very able British delegates at the Congress; Rosika Schwimmer, politically a Hungarian, but to whom nothing human is alien; Madam Ramondt-Hirschman, one of the most active of the hospitable and capable Dutch women who prepared the way for the Congress; and myself, coming from the United States. Grace Wales, a Canadian, the author of the well-known pamphlet "*Continuous Mediation without Armistice,*" also went with us to the Scandinavian countries, nominally as our secretary.

The natural route from Amsterdam to Copenhagen is overland through Germany to Warnemünde. To be sure, under war conditions with no night trains, it takes two days, with an over-night stop at Hamburg, but this was the least of the difficulty. Our two British friends could not cross "enemy" territory, and to find a boat was not easy. When found, it was a little freighter, with no cabin but the captain's, no woman on board, inconvenient in every way.

As only one passenger could go on the boat, it was decided Miss Wales should go ahead, this delay leaving Miss Macmillan a week more for work on the very difficult task of preparing our polyglot proceedings for a printer whose proof-setting and proof-reading customs were entirely strange to us.

The other three of us went by train through fields with thriving crops and few men-folk, over heaths where prisoners of war were at work converting the moor into ploughland, past station platforms where fathers and wives were bidding sad good-bys to their soldier boys, and where girls with the red cross on their arms were serving refreshments to passing troops.

In Copenhagen we were welcomed by our Hague friends, photographed, interviewed, fêted. While all this has its value, as it gives occasion for discussing peace issues and for knitting international ties, our mission was a formal one. We were accordingly very glad when arrangements were completed for an interview with Prime Minister Zahle, and Minister of Foreign Affairs Scavenius. Immediately after the interview we left for Norway.

In Christiania our programme was even fuller. Our first interview was with King Haakon VII, who kept us so long that we began to fear that, in our ignorance of ceremonial, we had missed the signal which ends a royal reception. Only at the end of an hour and three-quarters it came. The talk was wide-ranging, yet it ever centred about the war. The King appeared to be deeply interested in our mediation plan. He spoke with evident satisfaction of Norway's equal suffrage.

We went directly from the King to the Minister of Foreign Affairs, Ihlen, and later were given an appointment with Knudsen, the Prime Minister. We were also given what is, we were told, the most formal recognition that can be given to unofficial persons, being received in the Parliament House by the four presidents of the *Storting* or Parliament—President Castberg, president of the *Odelsting* (one of the two coördinate chambers), and a member of the Norwegian interparliamentary group; President Jahren, president of the *Lagting;* President Aarsbad, president of the *Storting* when meeting in joint session; and Vice-President Lövland. We were interested in seeing on the walls the portrait of the first woman member of Parliament.

At a committee meeting at the Nobel Institute we had an opportunity to discuss peace programmes with Christian Lange, secretary of the Interparliamentary Union.

In Stockholm, whither we proceeded at once, we had a very interesting interview with Wallenberg, the foreign minister. He is not only a statesman but a man of affairs and a great banker, and appears to be throwing all his weight on the side of peace.

Among distinguished Swedes who showed their sympathy and interest, at one of the meetings arranged for us we were proud to number Selma Lagerlöf.

We had already spent over a fortnight upon our way when, on the evening of June 7, we started for Russia. At this point we had to make certain changes. Rosika Schwimmer, being technically an enemy, could not go to Russia, and in her stead our Scandinavian friends chose for us Baroness Ellen Palmstierna. Madam Schwimmer, returning, went first to Denmark, where she took part in the great procession with which the Danish women celebrated the signing of the new constitution securing equal suffrage to Denmark.

The usual route from Stockholm to Petrograd is across the narrow seas to Abö in Finland. This passage is now closed to travellers, which means that one must make a railroad journey of three days and three nights round the head of the Gulf of Bothnia. We had been told that this journey would be very hard travelling, but we did not find it so, although we were glad to reach the Hotel Astoria in Petrograd a little before midnight on June 10. We stayed here an unexpectedly long time,—a fortnight, in fact,—and this gave us opportunity to see much of this fine and interesting capital, filled to-day with Red Cross "lazarets" and with wounded; a clean, orderly, and friendly city, as we observed it.

Our object was an interview with Sazonoff, Minister of Foreign Affairs, and it was a memorable experience to sit for nearly an hour in conference with one who has so large a part in the making of history in this tragic crisis. He appeared to be already familiar with the resolutions passed at The Hague, and interested to consider them with us.

Our return trip took us, on practically the longest day of the year, to the farthest point of our journey, well to the north of Archangel. Here, although in the vicissitudes of woods and hills we could not command the horizon, we had the pleasure of seeing the sun well risen before twelve minutes after midnight. It was probably below the horizon a scant twenty minutes.

In Stockholm we found that during our absence arrangements had been completed by the Swedish women for a wonderful set of simultaneous peace meetings. In three hundred and forty-three places, meetings were held on Sunday, June 27; at each the same speech—a very able one—was delivered and the same resolution passed. In spite of the fact of its being a season when people are scattered and meetings are thought to be impracticable, the demonstration which we attended gathered perhaps two thousand people, besides an overflow of some twelve hundred, while eight hundred could not get in at all. Yet this was only one of five meetings in Stockholm alone. The resolution affirmed the main resolutions of our Hague Congress, and called for mediation.

In the Scandinavian countries we saw ministers again on our return journey, and in Holland we had further interviews with Minister of Foreign Affairs Louden and the prime minister. It seemed best for Rosika Schwimmer and Mme. Ramondt to go again to Berlin, and for Chrystal Macmillan and me to visit London before I should return to America and report all this to President Wilson, as has now been done.

Our London fortnight was in some ways the most absorbing of all. We met many interesting people, including the women of our own British Committee.

We saw, too, officers of the National Peace Council; and of the League of Peace and Freedom; the chairman of the conference upon the Pacifist Philosophy of Life, held in London in July, and of the Fellowship of Reconciliation; members of the executive committee of the Representative Peace Conference, convened by the Society of Friends; and various members of the Union of Democratic Control.

We met many others, all were eager to hear of our undertaking, and with one or two marked exceptions, all were in their own way more or less distinctly pacifist in their outlook. I was conscious that they were far from reflecting average English feeling; yet, even so, what a testimony to the genuineness of English liberty of thought and the breadth of English humanism were their keen and generous views!

Two groups with whom I did not come into contact were the Stop the War Committee and the No Conscription Fellowship.

What was accomplished by the Hague Congress and the resulting undertakings, what their significance, is something that we do not yet fully know, ourselves. Five things stand out in my estimate of it all:

1. The noble humanity of the women who gathered at The Hague, all finding firm and common ground under their feet even in the midst of the war;
2. The well-wrought-out platform;

3. The permanent international pacifist organization of women, now effected;

4. A plan already under way for calling a congress of these women at the time and place where peace terms are being agreed on, when that time comes;

5. The mission to the Governments, in its immediate and remoter bearings.

I want to say a few words more regarding these last three points. And first as to permanent organization of women's work for durable peace. The new international headquarters at 467 Keizersgracht, Amsterdam, are but the symbol of the organization which women are eagerly forming everywhere. In all countries national groups of the International Women's Committee for Permanent Peace are being organized—in France (where at first there was considerable misunderstanding about the movement), in Germany, in Hungary, in England, in the Scandinavian countries, and in Russia. The American office is the national headquarters of the Women's Peace Party in Chicago.

Money and workers are needed and America, unstricken by war, must do more than its share. Its fair share, even, is a large one. The work already done has cost considerable sums, although many of the delegates, including all of those from the United States, paid all their own travelling expenses and contributed as well to the general expenses of the Congress. The future offers opportunity for still larger investments.

The coming Peace Congress of women must be planned and financed. This is my second point. Peace negotiations may come early and unexpectedly or, alas, they may be delayed for years; but sometime, come they must. And then the women must gather to note, to discuss, and to urge terms of peace, as contrasted with terms of a short-sighted armistice based on log-rolling politics. Professor LaFontaine of Belgium said to me recently that he considered the preparations for this future Congress, which were laid at The Hague, as the most important part of our work there.

Of my last point, the mission to the Governments, it is too early to speak, both because the work is confidential and cannot be reported and because it is still in process. However, I may say that what was planned as a comparatively formal presentation of the resolutions of our Congress developed into something more than this. Never again must women dare to believe that they are without responsibility because they are without power. Public opinion is power; strong and reasonable feeling is power; determination, which is a twin sister of faith or vision, is power. When our unaccustomed representatives knocked at the doors of the Chancelleries of Europe, there was not one but opened. They were received gravely, kindly, perhaps gladly, by twenty-one ministers, the presidents of two republics, a king, and the Pope. All, apparently, recognized without argument that an expression of the public opinion of a large body of women had every claim to consideration in questions of war and peace.

6

The Time for Making Peace

EMILY G. BALCH

✍ There is a widespread feeling that this is not the moment to talk of a European peace. On the contrary, if we look into the matter more deeply, there are good reasons to believe that the psychological moment is very close upon us. If, in the wisdom that comes after the event, we see that the United States was dilatory when it might have helped to open the way to end bloodshed and to make a fair and lasting settlement, we shall have cause for deep self-reproach.

The question of peace is a question of terms. Every country desires peace at the earliest possible moment, if peace can be had on what it regards as satisfactory terms. Peace is possible whenever the moment comes when each side would accept what the other side would grant, but from the international or human point of view a satisfactory peace is possible only when these claims and concessions are such as to forward, not to hinder, human progress. If Germany's terms are the annexation of Belgium and part of France and a military hegemony over the rest of Europe, or if the terms of France or England include "wiping Germany off the map of Europe," then there is no possibility of peace at this time or at any time that can be foreseen, nor does the world desire peace on these terms.

In each country there are those that want to continue the fight until military supremacy is achieved, in each there are powerful forces that seek a settlement of the opposite type, one which instead of containing within itself the threats to international stability that are involved in annexation, humiliation of the enemy, and competition between armaments, shall secure national independence and respect for rights of minorities, and foster international coöperation.

In one sense the present war is a war between the two great sets of belligerent powers, in another and more significant sense, it is a struggle between two conceptions of national policy. The catchwords imperialism and democracy indicate briefly the two opposing ideas. In every country both are represented, though in varying proportions, and in every country there is a strife between them.

The overriding of the regular civil government by the military authorities in all the warring countries is one of the too little understood effects of the war. The forms of constitutionalism may be undisturbed but as *inter arma leges silent* so military power tends to control the representatives of the people none the less really because unobtrusively. Von Tirpitz, Kitchener, Joffre, the Grand Duke Nicholas have tended to overshadow their nominal rulers.

Another effect of war is that as between the two contending voices, one is presented with a megaphone and the other is muffled if not gagged. Papers and platforms are open to "patriotic" utterances as patriotism is understood by the jingoes; the moderate is silenced not alone by the censor, not alone by social pressure, but by his own sense of the effect abroad of all that gives an impression of internal division and a readiness to quit the fight. In our own country during the tension with Germany loyal Americans who believe that the case of the United States is not a strong one (and a hundred million people cannot all think alike on such an issue), those who loathe the idea of going to war cannot and will not seek any commensurate expression of their views for fear this may make it harder for our Government to induce Germany to render her naval warfare less inhuman.

Thus everywhere war gives an exaggerated influence to militaristic and jingo forces and creates a false impression of the pressure for extreme terms as a basis of settlement.

Each side, of course, would like to make peace when the struggle, which is in a rough general sense a stalemate, is marked by some incident favorable to itself. Germany would like to make peace from the crest of the wave of her invasion of Russia; Russia and England from a conquered Constantinople. If the disinterested neutrals, who alone are free to act for peace, wait for the moment when neither side has any advantage, they will wait long indeed. The minor ups and downs of the war are shifting and unpredictable, but their importance is much less than it appears. The gains that either makes are as nothing to its losses. The grim unquestioned permanent fact, which affects both sides and which is to the changing fortunes of battle as the miles of immovable ocean depths are to the waves on its surface,—this all-outweighing fact is the intolerable burden of continued war.

This fact is that which makes a momentary advantage comparatively unimportant. All the belligerents want peace; though they none of them want it enough to cry "I surrender," they all want it enough to be ready to treat.

The making of peace involves not only the questions of the character of the terms, of demands more or less extreme—it also involves the question of the principle according to which settlements are to be made. Here too there are two conflicting conceptions.

On the one hand there is the assumption that military advantage must be represented *quid pro quo* in the terms,—so much victory, so much corresponding advantage in the terms. There is even the commercial conception of war as an investment and the idea that the fighter has a right to indemnity for what he has spent.

On the other hand, starting from the fact that the war has thrown certain international adjustments into the melting pot, the problem is to create a new adjustment such as on the whole shall be as generally satisfactory and contain as much promise of stability as possible.

The gains won by force have no claims that anyone is bound to respect. The expenditure of blood and treasure is no basis for a demand for reimbursement, no one has contracted to render any return for it, and it is to the general interest that such expenditure, undertaken on speculation, should never prove a good investment. Admitting these things, yet since the arbitrament of war is an arbitrament of force, this fact is bound to tell in the resulting adjustment. But a fact that it is important to understand is that with a given balance of relative strength as between the two sides, an equilibrium may be reached in more than one way, as there are equations which admit of more than one solution. The equilibrium of peace might be secured by balancing unjust acquisition against unjust acquisition or by balancing magnanimous concession against magnanimous concession.

A mediator or mediating group, without throwing any weight into the scale of one or the other side, can help to find the equilibrium on the higher rather than the lower level. We find a parallel in the economic sphere when there is a choice between a balance based on low wages and low efficiency and one based on high wages and high efficiency and when the state, not interfering with the economic balance, yet helps to secure that balance by the socially desirable method.

On the basis of military advantage or on the basis of military costs the neutrals have no claim to be heard in the settlement. The soldier is genuinely aggrieved and outraged that they should mix in the matter at all. Yet, even on the plane of fighting power, unexhausted neutrals are capable of throwing a sword into the scale and on the plea of costs suffered they have good claim to a voice. It is however as representatives of civilization and the true interests of all sides alike, that those who have not been in the thick of the conflict can and should be of use in the settlement and help to fix it on the higher plane.

The settlement of a war by outsiders—not their mere friendly coöperation in finding acceptable terms—is something that has often occurred, exhibiting that curious mixture of the crassest brute force with the most ambitious idealism which frequently characterizes the conduct of international dealings. The fruits of victory were refused to Russia by the Congress of Berlin in 1878, Europe recently denied to Japan the spoils of her war with China, the results of the Balkan wars were largely determined by those who had done none of the fighting. While mere physical might played a large part in such interferences from the outside, there is something besides hypocrisy in the claim of the statesmen of countries which had taken no part in a war to speak on behalf of freedom, progress, and peace.

A peace involving annexation of unwilling peoples could never be a lasting one. The widespread sense of irritation at all talk of peace at present seems to be due to a feeling that a settlement now would be a settlement which would leave Belgium, if not part of France, in German hands. Such a settlement would be as disastrous to Germany as to any nation. It might put an end to military operations, but it certainly would not bring peace, if we give any moral content to that much-abused word. Europe was not at peace before August, 1914, nor Poland for long before, nor Ireland, nor Alsace, nor Finland. Any community which, if it could, would fight to change its political status may be quiet under coercion, but it is not at peace. Neither would Europe be at peace with Germany in Belgium.

The question is, then, what sort of peace may we hope for now—on what terms, on what principles?

We may be sure that each side is ready to concede more and to demand less than appears on the surface or than it is ready to advertise. The summer campaign, in which marked advantages are most likely, once over, the belligerents are faced with a winter in the trenches which will cost on all sides, in money and in suffering, out of all proportion to the gains that can be hoped for. It must be remembered, too, that the advantages hitherto won are not all on one side, but that each side has something to concede. The British annexations of Egypt and Cyprus may be formal rather than substantial changes, but the conquest of Germany's colonies, large and small, Southwest Africa, Togo Land, Samoa, Neu-Pommern, Kaiser Wilhelm's Land, the Solomon, Caroline, and Marshall islands, to say nothing of Kiao-Chao—and probably Russian gains at the expense of Turkey in the East, give bargaining power to the allies. So, even without success in the Dardanelles, does their ability to thwart or forward German enterprise in Asia Minor and Mesopotamia or possibly in purchasable parts of Africa or elsewhere. Friends of Finland and of Poland must see to it that the debatable lands of the Eastern as well as of the Western front are kept in mind. From the point of view of Poland the main thing to be desired is the union of the three dismembered parts—Russian, German, and Austrian Poland—and their fusion in some sort of a buffer state, independent or at least essentially autonomous. Something like this appears to be the purpose of both Germany and Russia, with the difference that this Polish state would be in the one case under Teutonic, in the other under Russian auspices. No one knows, as between the two, which would be the choice of the majority of the Poles concerned. Concessions to Germany in Finland and in Poland, especially if coupled with adequate security from nationalistic oppression, might prove to be in the ultimate interest of European peace, and would render it easier for Germany to make the concession on her side of complete withdrawal in the West. Very important too are the concessions in regard to naval control of the seas that Great Britain ought to be willing to make if the safety of her commerce and her intercolonial communications could be secured otherwise, and this would seem to be the natural counterpart of substantiat steps toward disarmament on land.

But all this is speculation. The fact, obvious to those who look be-

low the surface, is that every belligerent power is carrying on a war dead-
ly to itself, that bankruptcy looms ahead, that industrial revolt threat-
ens, not at the moment but in a none too distant future, that racial stocks
are being irreparably depleted. The prestige of Europe, of the Christian
Church, of the white race, is lowered inch by inch with the progress of
the struggle which is continually closer to the *débâcle* of a civilization.

Each power would best like peace on its own terms, although our
common civilization would suffer by the imposition of extreme terms
by any power. Each power would be thankful indeed to secure an early
peace without humiliation on terms a long way short of its extreme
demands. There is every reason to believe that a vigorous initiative by
representatives of the neutral powers of the world could at this moment
begin a move toward negotiations, and lead the way to a settlement
which, please God, shall be a step toward a nobler and more intelligent
civilization than we have yet enjoyed.

7

Women and Internationalism

JANE ADDAMS

✍ The group of women from five of the European nations who, under the leadership of Dr. Aletta Jacobs of Amsterdam, convened the International Congress of Women at The Hague, were confident that although none of the existing international associations had met since the beginning of the war, the women, including those from the belligerent nations, would be able to come together in all sobriety and friendliness to discuss their common aims and the perilous stake they all held in the war.

The women who attended the Congress from the warring countries came from home at a moment when the individual, through his own overwhelming patriotism, fairly merges his personal welfare, his convictions, almost his sense of identity, into the national consciousness. It is a precious moment in human experience, almost worth the price of war, but it made the journey of the women leaving home to attend the Congress little short of an act of heroism. Even to appear to differ from those she loves in the hour of their affliction has ever been the supreme test of a woman's conscience.

For the women who came from neutral nations there were also great difficulties. In the Scandinavian countries women are enfranchised and for long months had been sensitive to the unusual international conditions which might so easily jeopardize the peace of a neutral nation and because in a large Congress an exaggerated word spoken, or reported as spoken, might easily make new complications, they too took risks and made a moral venture.

The fifteen hundred women who came to the Congress in the face of such difficulties must have been impelled by some profound and spiritual forces. During a year when the spirit of internationalism had apparently broken down, they came together to declare the validity of the internationalism which surrounds and completes national life, even as national life itself surrounds and completes family life; to insist that internationalism does not conflict with patriotism on one side any more than family devotion conflicts with it upon the other.

In the shadow of the intolerable knowledge of what war means, revealed so minutely during the previous months, these women also made solemn protest against that of which they knew. The protest may have been feeble, but the world progresses, in the slow and halting manner in which it does progress, only in proportion to the moral energy exerted by the men and women living in it; advance in international affairs, as elsewhere, must be secured by the human will and understanding united for conscious ends.

The delegates to the Congress were not without a sense of complicity in the war, and so aware of the bloodshed and desolation surrounding them that their deliberations at moments took on the solemn tone of those who talk around the bedside of the dying. It was intimated on the floor of the Congress that the time may come when the exhausted survivors of the war may well reproach women for their inaction during this year. It is possible they may then say that when a perfervid devotion to the ideals of patriotism drove thousands of men into international warfare, the women refused to accept the challenge for the things of the spirit and in that moment of terror they too failed to assert the supreme sanctity of human life. We were told that wounded lads, lying in helpless pain and waiting too long for the field ambulance, call out constantly for their mothers, impotently beseeching them for help; of soldiers who say to their hospital nurses: "We can do nothing for ourselves but go back to the trenches so long as we are able. Cannot the women do something about this war? Are you kind to us only when we are wounded?" There is no one else to whom they dare so speak, revealing the heart of the little child which each man carries within his own even when it beats under a uniform.

The belief that a woman is against war simply because she is a woman and not a man cannot of course be substantiated. In every country there are women who believe that war is inevitable and righteous; the majority of women as well as men in the nations at war doubtless hold that conviction. On the other hand, quite as an artist in an artillery corps commanded to fire upon a beautiful building like the *duomo* at Florence would be deterred by a compunction unknown to the man who had never given himself to creating beauty and did not know the intimate cost of it, so women, who have brought men into the world and nurtured them until they reach the age for fighting, must experience a peculiar revulsion when they see them destroyed, irrespective of the country in which these men may have been born.

Perhaps the most pathetic women we met, either at the Congress or later, were those who had sent their sons and husbands into the war, having themselves ceased to believe in it. I remember one mother who said: "Yes, I lost my son in the first three months of the war and I am thankful he died early before he harmed the son of any other woman called an enemy." To another woman, who as well as her husband was a pacifist, I said, "It must be hard for you and your husband to have lost a son in battle," and she replied quickly: "He did not die in battle, I am happy to say he never engaged in battle. He died of blood poisoning in one of the trenches, but we have reason to believe there had been no active engagement where he was stationed." The husband of another woman had gone to the front, telling her that under no circumstances would he be driven to kill a fellow man. One night he met a sentry from whom she believes he might have defended himself but he lost his life rather than put another man out of existence.

It was also said at the Congress that the appeals for the organization of the world upon peaceful lines may have been made too exclusively to reason and a sense of justice, that reason is only a part of the human endowment; emotion and deep-set racial impulses must be utilized as well—those primitive human urgings to foster life and to protect the helpless of which women were the earliest custodians and even the social and gregarious instincts that we share with the animals themselves. These universal desires must be given opportunities to expand and to have a recognized place in the formal organization of international relations which up to this moment have rested so exclusively upon purely legal foundations in spite of the fact that international law is comparatively undeveloped. There is an international commerce, a great system of international finance, and many other fields in which relationships are not yet defined in law, quite as many of our most settled national customs have never been embodied in law at all. It would be impossible to adjudicate certain of the underlying economic and social causes of this war according to existing international law and this might therefore make more feasible the proposition urged by the Women's Congress at The Hague, of a conference of neutral nations composed of men who have had international experience so long and so unconsciously that they have come to think not merely in the terms but in the realities of internationalism and would therefore readily deal with the economic and human element involved in the situation. Such a conference would represent not one country or another, but human experience as it has developed during the last decades in Europe. It would stand not for "peace at any price," but would seriously and painstakingly endeavor to discover the price to be paid for peace, which should if possible be permanent as well as immediate. The neutral nations might well say: "Standing outside, as we do, refusing to judge your cause, because that must be left to the verdict of history, we beg of you to remember that as life is being lived at this moment on this planet of ours, difficult and complicated situations must in the end be decided and adjudicated by the best minds and the finest good will that can be brought to bear upon them. We who are outside of this fury of fighting agree that you have all proven your valor, you have demonstrated the splendor of patriotism and of united action, but we beg of you, in the name of the humane values of life, in the name of those spiritual bonds you once venerated, to allow us to bring in some other method for ending the conflict. We believe that only through help from the outside will this curious spell be broken. Great and wonderful as the war has been in certain aspects, it cannot commend itself to the people of neutral nations who are striving to look at life rationally. It is certainly possible to give powers of negotiation to some body of men who, without guile and without personal or nationalistic ambitions, will bend their best energies to the task of adjudication."

A survey of the situation from the humane and social standpoint would consider for instance the necessity of feeding those people in the southeast portion of Europe who are pitifully underfed when there is a shortage of crops, in relation to the possession of warm-water harbors which would enable Russia to send them her great stores of wheat.

Such harbors would be considered not in their political significance, as when the blockade of the Bosphorus during the Tripolis War put a stop to the transport of crops from Odessa to the Mediterranean, not from a point of view of the claims of Russia nor the counterclaims of some other nation, but from the point of view of the needs of Europe. If men of such temper, experience, and understanding of life were to make propositions to the various Governments, not in order to placate the claims of one nation and to balance them against the claims of another, but from the human standpoint, there is little doubt but that the international spirit would again reassert itself and might eventually obtain a hearing. If the purely legalistic aspects were not overstressed, such a raising of the international standard would doubtless be reënforced in many ways. For centuries Europe has not been without a witness to the spiritual unity of nations. Pope Benedict XV, who gave our delegation an audience of half an hour, and Cardinal Gaspari, in an extended interview, made it evident that the men with religious responsibility fear keenly the results of this war; while the statesmen see in it a throwback to civilization, the great international Church views it as a breeder of animosities which will tear down and rend to pieces the work of years.

We also met in several countries the representatives of Protestant Churches organized into World Alliances or International Friendships, and countless individuals who could scarcely brook the horror of Jew fighting against Jew, Christian against Christian.

The International Congress of Women at The Hague passed a resolution to hold a meeting "in the same place and at the same time as the Conference of the Powers which shall frame the terms of the peace settlement after the war, for the purpose of presenting practical proposals to that Conference."[1] We recalled the fact that at the Congress of Vienna, held in 1815, in addition to determining by treaty the redistribution of the territory conquered by Napoleon, the slave trade was denounced and declared to be "contrary to the principles of civilization and human rights," although of course the abolition of slavery was a matter for each state to determine for itself.

1. The reader is referred to the official report of the International Congress of Women at The Hague for a fuller account of this resolution and the organization already effected for carrying out its provisions.

Within the borders of every country at war there is released a vast amount of idealism, without which war could never be carried on; a fund which might still be drawn upon when the time for settlement arrives. If the people knew that through final negotiations Europe would be so remade and internationalized that further wars would be impossible, many of them would feel that the death of thousands of young men had not been in vain, that the youth of our generation had thus contributed to the inauguration of a new era in human existence. It is, therefore, both because of the precedent in 1815 and at other times of peace negotiations when social reforms have been considered, and because idealism runs high in the warring nations, that the women in the Hague Congress considered it feasible to urge a declaration that "the exclusion of women from citizenship is contrary to the principles of civilization and human right," as one of the fundamental measures embodied in their resolutions for permanent peace.

But perhaps our hopes for such action are founded chiefly upon the fact that the settlement at the end of this war may definitely recognize a fundamental change in the functions of government taking place in all civilized nations, a change evoked as the result of concrete, social, and economic conditions, approximating similarity all over the world. The recent entrance of women into citizenship coming on so rapidly not only in the nations of Europe and America, but discernible in certain Asiatic nations as well, is doubtless one manifestation of this change, and the so-called radical or progressive element in each nation, whether they like it or not, recognize it as such. Nevertheless, there are men in each of these countries even among those who would grant the franchise to women in city and state, to whom it is still repugnant that women should evince an interest in international affairs. These men argue that a woman's municipal vote may be cast for the regulation of contagious diseases, her state vote for protection of working children, and that war no longer obtains between cities or even between states; but because war is still legitimate in settling international difficulties, and because international relations are so much a matter of fortified boundaries and standing armies, that it is preposterous for women who cannot fight, to consider them. Furthermore, when war was practically man's sole occupation, no one had a voice in the deliberations of the nation save those responsible for its defence, the king, the nobles, the knights. In the succeeding centuries, as other tests of social utility have been developed and the primitive test of fighting has subsided, the electorate has been steadily enlarged, the *bourgeoisie,* the working man, and last the woman, each group largely following its own interests as government took them over,—the regulation of commercial relations, of industrial conditions, of the health and education of children. Only in time of war is government thrown back to its primitive and sole function of self-defence, belittling for the moment the many other real interests of which it is the guardian. War moreover has always treated the lives of men and women broadly, as a landscape painter who suppresses all details—"The man bold, combative, conquering; woman sympathetic, healing the wounds that war has made."

But because this primitive conception of the function of government and of the obsolete division between the lives of men and women has obtained during the long months of the European war, there is obviously great need at the end of the war that women should attempt, in an organized capacity, to make their contribution to that governmental internationalism between the nations which shall in some measure approximate the genuine internationalism already developed in so many directions among the peoples. In normal times, moreover, all modern Governments with any living relation to the great developments in commerce, industry, sanitary science, or a dozen other aspects of contemporary life, are coming to realize that the current type of government implies the frequent subordination of an isolated nationalism to general international interests. It is hoped that this new approach to international relationships, typified by the international postal system and a hundred other semi-governmental regulations, will be vital enough to assert itself at the end of this war as over against the militaristic and "armed peace" relationships.

An organized and formal effort on the part of women would add but one more to that long procession of outstanding witnesses who in each generation have urged juster and more vital international relations between Governments. Each exponent in this long effort to place law above force was called a dreamer and a coward, but each did his utmost to express clearly the truth that was in him, and beyond that human effort cannot go.

This tide of endeavor has probably never been so full as at the present moment. Religious, social, and economic associations, many of them organized since the war began, are making their contributions to the same great end. Several of them are planning to meet at "the Conference of the Powers which shall frame the terms of the peace settlement after this war," and such meetings are not without valuable precedent.

A federation or a council of European powers should not be considered impossible from the very experience of the nations now at war. The German Empire, Consolidated Italy, or the United Kingdom have been evolved from separate states which had previously been at war with each other during centuries; the response to the call of imperialistic England, during the last months, for more troops has shown that patriotic emotion can be extended to include the Boers of South Africa and the natives of India; certain of these great federated states and empires have again formed alliances with each other and are fighting together against a common enemy.

Is it too much to hope that the good will and the consciousness of common aims and responsibilities can be extended to include all the European nations and that devices for international government can be provided, able to deal in the interests of the whole with each difficult situation as it arises? The very experience of this war should demonstrate its feasibility and the analogy inevitably suggests itself that as the states of Germany and Italy came together under the pressure of war, possibly this larger federation may be obtained under the same sense of united effort.

Out of the present situation, which certainly "presents the spectacle of the breakdown of the whole philosophy of nationalism, political, racial, and cultural," may conceivably issue a new birth of internationalism, founded not so much upon arbitration treaties, to be used in time of disturbance, as upon governmental devices designed to protect and enhance the fruitful processes of coöperation in the great experiment of living together in a world become conscious of itself.

Appendix 1

Opinions of the Congress

". . . The deliberations of the Congress of Women at The Hague was the appeal away from passion and insane hatred to balance of judgment and to truth inspired by reason.

"A visitor who sat in the gallery was impressed by the similarity in personality and dress of the delegates who occupied the body of the hall. There was nothing in general appearance to distinguish one nationality from another, and looking into our own hearts we beheld as in a mirror the hearts of all those who were assembled with us, because deep in our own hearts lies the common heart of humanity. We realised that the fear and mistrust that had been fostered between the peoples of the nations was an illusion. We discovered that at the bottom peace was nothing more or less than communal love. There could be nothing negative in the idea of peace. War is the negative. Peace is the highest effort of the human brain applied to the organisation of the life and being of the peoples of the world on the basis of coöperation. It cannot be secured with treaties or maintained by armaments; it must be founded ultimately on the public opinion of enlightened and free democracies knit together by organised association in common ideals and common enterprises.

"It was to the furtherance of such an ideal that the representatives of the Women's Congress pledged their strenuous and passionate endeavour.

"London.

"Emmeline Pethick Lawrence."

✍

"It seems ludicrous to imagine that there is one woman in the world presumptuous enough to believe that an international women's congress could end this maddest of all wars. What did we intend then? I hear our opponents ask.

"To protest against the useless destruction of the highest fruits of civilisation.

"To protest against this human slaughter.

"To protest against the mad national hatred.

"To protest against the war and all its accompaniment.

"To protest not only with words, but with deeds; and this Congress was a deed. . . .

"But what did the Congress give to those of us who took part in it? I cannot know what it gave to others, only what it gave to me personally. The days in The Hague were a rest after months of anguish—a rest amongst those who felt the same. The days in The Hague gave me an answer to the question which I had asked myself since the outbreak of war in anxious days and weary nights: Where are the women? They were here! United in energetic protest, penetrated with warm humanity, inspired by one thought—to do their duty as wives and mothers, to protect life, to fight against national hatred, to guard civilisation, to further justice—justice not only for their own country, but for all countries of the world. The days in The Hague gave fresh courage for new activity.

"Munich.

"LIDA GUSTAVA HEYMANN."

Appendix 2

Some Particulars about the Congress

How the Congress Was Called

The scheme of an International Congress of Women was formulated at a small conference of Women from neutral and belligerent countries, held at Amsterdam, early in Febr. 1915. A preliminary programme was drafted at this meeting, and it was agreed to request the Dutch Women to form a Committee to take in hand all the arrangement for the Congress and to issue the invitations.

Finance

The expenses of the Congress were guaranteed by British, Dutch and German Women present who all agreed to raise one third of the sum required.

Membership

Invitations to take part in the Congress were sent to women's organisations and mixed organisations as well as to individual women all over the world. Each organisation was invited to appoint two delegates.

Women only could become members of the Congress and they were required to express themselves in general agreement with the resolutions on the preliminary programme. This general agreement was interpreted to imply the conviction *(a)* That international disputes should be settled by pacific means; *(b)* That the parliamentary franchise should be extended to women.

Conditions of Debate

The Congress was carried on under two important rules:

1. That discussions on the relative national responsibility for or conduct of the present war,
2. Resolutions dealing with the rules under which war shall in future be carried on, shall be outside the scope of the Congress.

Countries Represented

The United States of America, which sent 47 members; Sweden, which sent 12; Norway, 12; Netherlands, 1,000; Italy, 1; Hungary, 9; Germany, 28; Denmark, 6; Canada, 2; Belgium, 5; Austria, 6, and Great Britain, 3, although 180 others from there were prevented from sailing owing to the closing of the North Sea for military reasons.

The Congress, which was attended by a large number of visitors as well as by the members, was extremely successful. Proceedings were conducted with the greatest goodwill throughout, and the accompanying resolutions were passed at the business sessions.

International Committee of the Congress

Austria.
>   Leop. Kulka,
>   Olga Misar
Belgium.
>   Eugénie Hamer,
>   Marguérite Sarten
Denmark.
>   Thora Daugaard,
>   Clara Tybjerg
Germany.
>   Dr. Anita Augspurg,
>   Lida Gustava Heymann,
>   *Secretary & Interpreter*
Great Britain and Ireland.
>   Chrystal Macmillan,
>   *Secretary,*
>   Kathleen Courtney,
>   *Interpreter*

Hungary.
    VILMA GLÜCKLICH,
    ROSIKA SCHWIMMER
Italy.
    ROSE GENONI,
    DR. ALETTA JACOBS
Netherlands
    HANNA VAN BIEMA-HYMANS,
      Secretary,
    DR. MIA BOISSEVAIN
Norway
    DR. EMILY ARNESEN,
    LOUISA KEILHAU
Sweden
    ANNA KLEMAN,
    EMMA HANSSON
U.S.A.
    JANE ADDAMS, *President,*
    FANNIE FERN ANDREWS

Appendix 3

Resolutions[1] Adopted by the International Congress of Women at The Hague, May 1, 1915

I. Women and War

1. Protest

We women, in International Congress assembled, protest against the madness and the horror of war, involving as it does a reckless sacrifice of human life and the destruction of so much that humanity has laboured through centuries to build up.

2. Women's Sufferings in War

This International Congress of Women opposes the assumption that women can be protected under the conditions of modern warfare. It protests vehemently against the odious wrongs of which women are the victims in time of war, and especially against the horrible violation of women which attends all war.

II. Action towards Peace

3. The Peace Settlement

This International Congress of Women of different nations, classes, creeds and parties is united in expressing sympathy with the suffering of all, whatever their nationality, who are fighting for their country or labouring under the burden of war.

Since the mass of the people in each of the countries now at war believe themselves to be fighting, not as aggressors but in self-defence and

1. The discussion of these Resolutions and others which were not carried is to be found in the official report of the International Congress of Women at The Hague.

for their national existence, there can be no irreconcilable differences between them, and their common ideals afford a basis upon which a magnanimous and honourable peace might be established. The Congress therefore urges the Governments of the world to put an end to this bloodshed, and to begin peace negotiations. It demands that the peace which follows shall be permanent and therefore based on principles of justice, including those laid down in the resolutions[2] adopted by this Congress, namely:

That no territory should be transferred without the consent of the men and women in it, and that the right of conquest should not be recognized.

That autonomy and a democratic parliament should not be refused to any people.

That the Governments of all nations should come to an agreement to refer future international disputes to arbitration or conciliation and to bring social, moral and economic pressure to bear upon any country which resorts to arms.

That foreign politics should be subject to democratic control.

That women should be granted equal political rights with men.

4. Continuous Mediation

This International Congress of Women resolves to ask the neutral countries to take immediate steps to create a conference of neutral nations which shall without delay offer continuous mediation. The Conference shall invite suggestions for settlement from each of the belligerent nations and in any case shall submit to all of them simultaneously, reasonable proposals as a basis of peace.

III. Principles of a Permanent Peace

5. Respect for Nationality

This International Congress of Women, recognizing the right of the people to self-government, affirms that there should be no[3] transference of territory without the consent of the men and women residing therein, and urges that autonomy and a democratic parliament should not be refused to any people.

---

2. The Resolutions in full are Nos. 5, 6, 7, 8, 9.

3. The Congress declared by vote that it interpreted no transference of territory without the consent of the men and women in it to imply that the right of conquest was not to be recognized.

6. Arbitration and Conciliation

This International Congress of Women, believing that war is the negation of progress and civilisation, urges the governments of all nations to come to an agreement to refer future international disputes to arbitration and conciliation.

7. International Pressure

This International Congress of Women urges the governments of all nations to come to an agreement to unite in bringing social; moral and economic pressure to bear upon any country, which resorts to arms instead of referring its case to arbitration or conciliation.

8. Democratic Control of Foreign Policy

Since war is commonly brought about not by the mass of the people, who do not desire it, but by groups representing particular interests, this International Congress of Women urges that Foreign Politics shall be subject to Democratic Control; and declares that it can only recognise as democratic a system which includes the equal representation of men and women.

9. The Enfranchisement of Women

Since the combined influence of the women of all countries is one of the strongest forces for the prevention of war, and since women can only have full responsibility and effective influence when they have equal political rights with men, this International Congress of Women demands their political enfranchisement.

IV. International Coöperation

10. Third Hague Conference

This International Congress of Women urges that a third Hague Conference be convened immediately after the war.

11. International Organization

This International Congress of Women urges that the organization of the Society of Nations should be further developed on the basis of a constructive peace, and that it should include:

a. As a development of the Hague Court of Arbitration, a permanent International Court of Justice to settle questions or differences of a justiciable character, such as arise on the interpretation of treaty rights or of the law of nations.

b. As a development of the constructive work of the Hague Conference, a permanent International Conference holding regular meetings in which women should take part, to deal not with the rules of warfare but with practical proposals for further International Coöperation among the States. This Conference should be so constituted that it could formulate and enforce those principles of justice, equity and good will in accordance with which the struggles of subject communities could be more fully recognized and the interests and rights not only of the great Powers and small nations but also those of weaker countries and primitive peoples gradually adjusted under an enlightened international public opinion.

This International Conference shall appoint:

A permanent Council of Conciliation and Investigation for the settlement of international differences arising from economic competition, expanding commerce, increasing population and changes in social and political standards.

12. General Disarmament

The International Congress of Women, advocating universal disarmament and realizing that it can only be secured by international agreement, urges, as a step to this end, that all countries should, by such an international agreement, take over the manufacture of arms and munitions of war and should control all international traffic in the same. It sees in the private profits accruing from the great armament factories a powerful hindrance to the abolition of war.

13. Commerce and Investments

a. The International Congress of Women urges that in all countries there shall be liberty of commerce, that the seas shall be free and the trade routes open on equal terms to the shipping of all nations.

b. Inasmuch as the investment by capitalists of one country in the resources of another and the claims arising therefrom are a fertile source of international complications, this International Congress of Women urges the widest possible acceptance of the principle that such investments shall be made at the risk of the investor, without claim to the official protection of his government.

14. National Foreign Policy

a. This International Congress of Women demands that all secret treaties shall be void and that for the ratification of future treaties, the participation of at least the legislature of every government shall be necessary.

b. This International Congress of Women recommends that National Commissions be created, and International Conferences convened for the scientific study and elaboration of the principles and conditions of permanent peace, which might contribute to the development of an International Federation.

These Commissions and Conferences should be recognized by the Governments and should include women in their deliberations.

15. Women in National and International Politics

This International Congress of Women declares it to be essential, both nationally and internationally to put into practice the principle that women should share all civil and political rights and responsibilities on the same terms as men.

V. The Education of Children

16. This International Congress of Women urges the necessity of so directing the education of children that their thoughts and desires may be directed towards the ideal of constructive peace.

VI. Women and the Peace Settlement Conference

17. This International Congress of Women urges, that in the interests of lasting peace and civilisation the Conference which shall frame the Peace settlement after the war should pass a resolution affirming the need in all countries of extending the parliamentary franchise to women.

18. This International Congress of Women urges that representatives of the people should take part in the conference that shall frame the peace settlement after the war, and claims that amongst them women should be included.

VII. Action to Be Taken

19. Women's Voice in the Peace Settlement

This International Congress of Women resolves that an international meeting of women shall be held in the same place and at the same time as the Conference of the Powers which shall frame the terms of the peace settlement after the war for the purpose of presenting practical proposals to that Conference.

20. Envoys to the Governments

In order to urge the Governments of the world to put an end to this bloodshed and to establish a just and lasting peace, this International Congress of Women delegates envoys to carry the message expressed in the Congress Resolutions to the rulers of the belligerent and neutral nations of Europe and to the President of the United States.

These Envoys shall be women of both neutral and belligerent nations, appointed by the International Committee of this Congress. They shall report the result of their missions to the International Committee of Women for permanent Peace as a basis for further action.

Appendix 4

Manifesto Issued by Envoys of the International Congress of Women at The Hague to the Governments of Europe and the President of the United States

Here in America, on neutral soil, far removed from the stress of the conflict we, the envoys to the Governments from the International Congress of Women at The Hague, have come together to canvass the results of our missions. We put forth this statement as our united and deliberate conclusions.

At a time when the foreign offices of the great belligerents have been barred to each other, and the public mind of Europe has been fixed on the war offices for leadership, we have gone from capital to capital and conferred with the civil governments.

Our mission was to place before belligerent and neutral alike the resolutions of the International Congress of Women held at The Hague in April; especially to place before them the definite method of a conference of neutral nations as an agency of continuous mediation for the settlement of the war.

To carry out this mission two delegations were appointed, which included women of Great Britain, Hungary, Italy, the Netherlands, Sweden, and the United States. One or other of these delegations were received by the governments in fourteen capitals, Berlin, Berne, Budapest, Christiania, Copenhagen, The Hague, Havre (Belgian Government), London, Paris, Petrograd, Rome, Stockholm, Vienna, and Washington. We were received by the Prime Ministers and Foreign Ministers of the Powers, by the King of Norway, by the Presidents of Switzerland and of the United States, by the Pope and the Cardinal Secretary of State. In many capitals more than one audience was given, not merely to present our resolutions, but for a thorough discussion. In addition to the thirty-five governmental visits we met—everywhere—members of parliaments and other leaders of public opinion.

We heard much the same words spoken in Downing Street as those spoken in Wilhelmstrasse, in Vienna, as in Petrograd, in Budapest, as in the Havre, where the Belgians have their temporary government.

Our visits to the war capitals convinced us that the belligerent Governments would not be opposed to a conference of neutral nations; that while the belligerents have rejected offers of mediation by single neutral nations, and while no belligerent could ask for mediation, the creation of a continuous conference of neutral nations might provide the machinery which would lead to peace. We found that the neutrals on the other hand were concerned, lest calling such a conference might be considered inopportune by one or other of the belligerents. Here our information from the belligerents themselves gave assurance that such initiative would not be resented. "My country would not find anything unfriendly in such action by the neutrals," was the assurance given us by the foreign Minister of one of the great belligerents. "My Government would place no obstacle in the way of its institution," said the Minister of an opposing nation. "What are the neutrals waiting for?" said a third, whose name ranks high not only in his own country, but all over the world.

It remained to put this clarifying intelligence before the neutral countries. As a result the plan of starting mediation through the agency of a continuous conference of the neutral nations is to-day being seriously discussed alike in the Cabinets of the belligerent and neutral countries of Europe and in the press of both.

We are in a position to quote some of the expressions of men high in the councils of the great nations as to the feasibility of the plan. "You are right," said one Minister, "that it would be of the greatest importance to finish the fight by early negotiation rather than by further military efforts, which would result in more and more destruction and irreparable loss." "Yours is the sanest proposal that has been brought to this office in the last six months," said the Prime Minister of one of the larger countries.

We were also in position to canvass the objections that have been made to the proposal, testing it out severely in the judgment of those in the midst of the European conflict. It has been argued that it is not the time at present to start such a process of negotiations, and that no step should be taken until one or other party has a victory, or at least until some new military balance is struck. The answer we bring is that every delay makes more difficult the beginnings of negotiations, more nations become involved, and the situation becomes more complicated; that when at times in the course of the war such a balance was struck, the neutrals were unprepared to act. The opportunity passed. For the forces of peace to be unprepared when the hour comes, is as irretrievable as for a military leader to be unready.

It has been argued that for such a conference to be called at any time when one side has met with some military advantage, would be to favor that side. The answer we bring is that the proposed conference would start mediation at a higher level than that of military advantage. As to the actual military situation, however, we quote a remark made to us by a foreign Minister of one of the belligerent Powers. "Neither side is to-day strong enough to dictate terms, and neither side is so weakened that it has to accept humiliating terms."

It has been suggested that such a conference would bind the neutral governments coöperating in it. The answer we bring is that, as proposed, such a conference should consist of the ablest persons of the neutral countries, assigned not to problems of their own governments, but to the common service of a supreme crisis. The situation calls for a conference cast in a new and larger mould than those of conventional diplomacy, the governments sending to it persons drawn from social, economic, and scientific fields who have had genuine international experience.

As women, it was possible for us, from belligerent and neutral nations alike, to meet in the midst of war and to carry forward an interchange of question and answer between capitals which were barred to each other. It is now our duty to make articulate our convictions. We have been convinced that the governments of the belligerent nations would not be hostile to the institution of such a common channel for good offices; and that the governments of the European neutrals we visited stand ready to coöperate with others in mediation. Reviewing the situation, we believe that of the five European neutral nations visited, three are ready to join in such a conference, and that two are deliberating the calling of such a conference. Of the intention of the United States we have as yet no evidence.

We are but the conveyors of evidence which is a challenge to action by the neutral governments visited—by Denmark, Holland, Norway, Sweden, Switzerland, and the United States. We in turn bear evidence of a rising desire and intention of vast companies of people in the neutral countries to turn a barren disinterestedness into an active good-will. In Sweden, for example, more than 400 meetings were held in one day in different parts of the country, calling on the government to act.

The excruciating burden of responsibility for the hopeless continuance of this war no longer rests on the wills of the belligerent nations alone. It rests also on the will of those neutral governments and people who have been spared its shock but cannot, if they would, absolve themselves from their full share of responsibility for the continuance of war.

Signed by

ALETTA JACOBS [Holland].
CHRYSTAL MACMILLAN [Great Britain].
ROSIKA SCHWIMMER [Austro-Hungary].
EMILY G. BALCH [United States].
JANE ADDAMS [United States].

Appendix 5

International Plan for Continuous Mediation without Armistice

JULIA GRACE WALES

*Delegate from the University of Wisconsin to the
International Congress of Women at The Hague*

Definition

The International Plan for Continuous Mediation without Armistice suggests that an International Commission of experts be formed, to sit as long as the war continues. The members of the commission should have a scientific but no diplomatic function; they should be without power to commit their governments. The Commission should explore the issues involved in the present struggle, and in the light of this study begin making propositions to the belligerents in the spirit of constructive internationalism. If the first effort fail, they should consult and deliberate, revise their original propositions or offer new ones, coming back again and again if necessary, in the unalterable conviction that some proposal will ultimately be found that will afford a practical basis for actual peace negotiation. The Commission should be established without delay, on neutral initiative.

Condensed Argument

Our argument for Continuous Mediation without Armistice rests on the following convictions:

(1) That humanity should be able to find some method of avoiding prolonged wholesale destruction;

(2) That on both sides there are people who believe themselves to be fighting in self-defense, who desire a right settlement, and who ought not to have to fight against each other; that it is an ultimate outrage against humanity that they have to do so;

(3) That the only way to straighten the tangle is to adopt and persistently employ the device of placing simultaneous conditional proposals ("will you—if the rest will?") before the belligerents; that neither side can think

correctly or effectively unless it has among the data of its thinking, exact knowledge as to how the enemy (not merely the government but the various elements of the people) would react to every possible proposal for settlement;

(4) That truth tends to work on the mind, and that to place sane standing proposals before the nations would tend to ripen the time for peace;

(5) That delay is dangerous because bitterness and the desire for revenge are growing stronger, and the civil power in all warring countries is daily growing weaker in proportion to the military;

(6) That there ought to be a commission of experts sitting throughout the war and in some way holding the possibilities of settlement before the belligerents; that world consciousness is trying to break through; that a world thinking organ should be created and that the creation of such an organ at this juncture would concentrate and render effective the idealism of all nations and open the possibility of establishing upon a deposed militarism, the beginnings of World-Federation.

The following objection has been raised against the neutral propaganda for Continuous Mediation without Armistice.

The neutral argument assumes that both sides are equally in the wrong— an assumption contrary to truth and hence fundamentally immoral.

In reply to this charge we emphatically assert that the neutral propaganda for Continuous Mediation without Armistice, makes no such assumption. What it does assume is that in any case there are some right-thinking people on both sides. In an appeal for coöperation to right-thinking people in all countries neutral and belligerent, whatever their national prejudices in connection with the present war, we believe that it would be out of place to dogmatize as to which side, if either, represents the cause of international righteousness for which we desire to contend, in working for the establishment of an international commission. We believe that any nation sincerely fighting for the right has nothing to fear from the plan and much to gain, that the Plan is on the side of any country that is on the side of international righteousness. We believe that the plan of Continuous Mediation without Armistice will tend to assist and reward right motives in every country and to thwart wrong motives. We believe that the citizen of any country understanding our plan and believing that his own country is fighting for the right will feel that the plan is favourable to his own national cause. We believe that the plan if carried out, would, while thwarting short-sighted national selfishness, tend to bring ultimate good to all lands—the genuine and permanent benefit which depends on the welfare of the family of nations as a whole. Among those working for the establishment of the International Commission are people of various national sympathies. Probably there is no one working for the establishment of the International Commission who has not a personal opinion as to which side on the whole represents the cause of right. We feel however, that difference of opinion as to the sincerity of the belligerents, the responsibility of the war, and the attitude which the various nations will take in the settlement need not prevent us from working together provided that we are agreed in our desire for the establishment of a permanent peace based on principles of international righteousness.

Index

Misar, Olga, 70
motherhood and sisterhood: activism linked to, xxiv–xxv; Addams's view of, xxx, 61; clear-thinking linked to, xxvi
Mott, John, xxxiv

National American Woman Suffrage Association, ix
National Conference of Charities and Correction (later, National Conference of Social Work), ix
national consciousness: generational gap in, 29–33; individual subsumed under, 59–60; use of term, 28. *See also* nationalism; patriotism
National Council of French Women, xvii
nationalism, 29–33, 66
nationality, 73
National Peace Council, 50
Netherlands: delegates from, 5–6, 7; envoys' visit to, 12, 50; interned soldiers in, 35
neutral nations: armaments and, xix–xx; as negotiators, 15; peace role of, xxvii, 44–46, 55–56; proposed conference of, 62–63; timing of negotiations and, 54–55; United States as, xi, 13, 15–16; women delegates from, 10, 59
Nobel Institute, 48
Nobel Peace Prize, xxxiv–xxxv
No Conscription Fellowship, 50
Norway: delegates from, 6; envoys' visit to, 48

O'Reilly, Leonora, 7
Osler, Willima, 25

pacifism: Addams on, x–xi; conference on, 50; in France, 22, 23, 24;

French women's manifesto on, xvii; in Germany, 14; in Great Britain, 25; in Hungary, 20–21; patriotism linked to, 28
Palmstierna, Ellen, xxv, xxxvii, 49
Palthe, Wollften, 12
patriotism: fanatical type of, xxviii, 40–41; generational gap in defining, 29–33; internationalism possible with, 60; jingoistic version of, 54; pacificism linked to, 28
peace: definition of, vii; desires for, 54–55; as focus of Congress, 6, 67; means of achieving, xx–xxi, 36–38; reasons for, 61–62; resolutions on permanent, 73–74, 76; time for, 53–58
peace advocates: cooperation among, 10–11; different approaches to, xviii–xix; following Hague congress, xxxi–xxxv; goals of, xi–xii; heroism of, 59–60; isolation of, 41–43; leadership of, viii–xiv; model for, x–xi; origins of, vii
peace settlement process: help in starting, xxx; idealism and, 64; immediate need for, 37–38; military advantage and, 55–56; resolutions on, 72–74, 76; women's representation in, xx–xxi, 51–52, 63. *See also* Wisconsin Plan
People's Council of America for Democracy and Terms of Peace, xxxii–xxxiii
Perlen, Frida, xvi
Pethick-Lawrence, Emmeline: appeal by, xi; on armaments, xix; on Congress, xx, 67; mentioned, 7; travels of, xvi, 5
Poland: hopes of, 57
Post, Alice Fletcher, xviii
press: censorship of, 17, 19–20, 42–

JANE ADDAMS (1860–1935) was a social activist, a leading Progressive reformer, public speaker, author of many books of social criticism, and an original theorist who contributed to the development of American sociology and pragmatist philosophy. Her feminism, pacifism, and pragmatist experimentalism found concrete expression in the institutions she founded or to which she gave early support, including the Hull-House settlement in Chicago, the National Association for the Advancement of Colored People, the National American Woman Suffrage Association, the American Civil Liberties Union, and the Women's International League for Peace and Freedom. She was awarded the Nobel Peace Prize in 1931.

EMILY GREENE BALCH (1867–1961), a social reformer and pacifist, taught economics at Wellesley College, where she served as professor and chair of the Department of Economics and Sociology. Among her published works is *Our Slavic Fellow Citizens* (1910) and *Occupied Haiti* (1927). She worked for the Women's International League for Peace and Freedom from its inception in 1919 until her retirement, writing many of the organization's position papers. She won the Nobel Peace Prize in 1946.

ALICE HAMILTON (1869–1970) held an M.D. degree from the University of Michigan and completed graduate work in bacteriology and pathology. Recognized as one of the first experts in the field of industrial toxicology, she led many efforts to improve health and safety in the workplace. Hamilton taught at Harvard Medical School and served as an investigator of occupational poisons for the U.S. Bureau of Labor Statistics. She was a resident at Hull-House for several years and a close friend of Jane Addams's until the latter's death.

Harriet Hyman Alonso is a professor of history at the City College of New York of the City University of New York. She is the author of many articles on women and peace and three books: *The Women's Peace Union and the Outlawry of War, 1921–1942* (1989, 1997), *Peace as a Women's Issue: A History of the U.S. Movement for World Peace and Women's Rights* (1993), and *Growing Up Abolitionist: The Story of the Garrison Children* (2002). She is a long-time member of the Peace History Society, serving as vice president and a member of the executive board. In 1996 she received the Bryant Spann Memorial (article) Prize from the Eugene V. Debs Foundation. Her book *Growing Up Abolitionist: The Story of the Garrison Children* received the Warren F. Kuehl Book Prize from the Society for Historians of American Foreign Relations in 2003.

The University of Illinois Press
is a founding member of the
Association of American University Presses.

Composed in 10.5/13 Minion
with Neuva display
by Jim Proefrock
at the University of Illinois Press
Designed by Copenhaver Cumpston
Manufactured by Cushing-Malloy, Inc.

University of Illinois Press
1325 South Oak Street
Champaign, IL 61820-6903
www.press.uillinois.edu